Now Listen
To
This

Now Listen To This

Building the House of Love

By Pastor Predest (Dwayne) Richardson

Xulon Press

Xulon Press
2301 Lucien Way #415
Maitland, FL 32751
407.339.4217
www.xulonpress.com

Unless otherwise indicated, Scripture quotations taken from
(Version(s) used)

Printed in the United States of America.

Edited by Xulon Press

ISBN-13: 9781545609415

Dedication

I WOULD LIKE to dedicate this book first, to my Lord and Savior, Jesus Christ, who has been sooooooo good to me in spite of me. Through his blood, He saved me from eternal damnation and gave me a new life and the hope of eternity with Him. I would like to further dedicate this book to my beautiful, loving, smiling, laughing wife, Brenda, who even smiles in her sleep. She has been sooooooo good to me and saved me from a life of destruction. Brenda has stuck with me through all my idiosyncrasies, obsessive compulsive behaviors, and sometimes eccentric ways. She has been a constant encouraging, driving force in my life, in our ministry, and in our walk with Christ. To my mother, Mildred (Jones) Campbell and my sister Aleta Jones, May you rest in peace.

Who gave himself for us, that he might redeem us from all iniquity, and purify unto himself a peculiar people, zealous of good works. Titus 2:14 (NIV)

Table of Contents

Introduction

I, PASTOR PREDEST Dwayne Richardson, do hereby solemnly swear that the words of this book are true. I further hereby declare that I am of sound mind, although many may beg to differ...sometimes myself included! I felt compelled to write this book because of the many miracles and blessings that I have witnessed after God called me into the ministry. He called me to rebuild a dilapidated church in Paulding, Ohio, which is an all-white community with only a handful of blacks. This is not a black against white book, nor do I mean to be offensive in my description of ethnicity and racial equality.

Why he would call me, I do not know. In the past, I have had difficulties maintaining a solid Christian life. I was always torn between living for God and living in the world. I struggled with fear, drugs, alcoholism, lust, honesty, and commitment (just to name a few). God is so multifaceted and omnipotent that he is able to turn anything around. He can work from the inside out, upside down, or bless your soul through the spirit of someone else who He touches. The work that I thought He was doing through me; He was doing TO me. GLORY TO GOD! My wife Brenda is by my side every step of the way.

Chapter 1

The History/Fear

I GREW UP on the west side of Chicago in an extended family household containing my mother, my maternal grandfather, my great grandmother, and my four sisters. It was a very difficult, yet liberating period in African-American history. Some of my earliest childhood memories include Dr. Martin Luther King Jr.'s assassination. I remember Chicago was on fire, and we sat on our back porch watching the flames reach the heavens. We wondered what was happening. My mother was crying and said, "Why did they have to do that to him?" My sister and I were sitting in our flannel pajamas, just staring at the scene before us.

As time went on I remember our next-door neighbor, he was gone for a long period of time, and then he returned. I was told that he had gone to a place called

Vietnam. He was a tall man who always had a big walking stick in his hand and a white German shepherd with him named Snowball. He wore his green military fatigues with the sleeves cut out, sporting a black tam on his head and a necklace revealing a black clenched fist around his neck symbolizing the Black Power movement. He didn't seem like the same neighbor I had known before. He talked and cursed to himself as he walked up and down the street. I remember seeing trucks driving around; they were regular three quarter ton trucks with railings supporting the flat bed. There were black men herded onto the back of these trucks, as if they were being hauled off to the stock yards. Two men would run alongside the truck. They grabbed any young men in the immediate area and beat them into submission until they boarded the trucks. I asked my friends what was going on and they said I better get in the house because they were initiating that night. I didn't know if it was initiation for the Black Panther Party or for the local gangs, but I knew there was something wrong with this.

The first time I remember feeling fear, I was about eight years old. Those same gangs would have wars. Gunshots would ring out all night as we would lie on the floor of our house, hoping for it to pass. We were not allowed to go to the windows. Most of the time, we would just lie on the floor until morning. When we woke we would walk through the house counting the bullet holes in the walls.

I also recall another first healthy fear I had. In our family, tradition was that during lightning storms my great grandmother would make us turn off all the electricity. She would then spread a patchwork quilt in the middle of the living room floor and there we would all lie quietly in the dim light of a flickering candle. We listened to her read the Bible to us for she was training us to fear the Lord. In African-American folklore, when it is lightning and thundering, God is speaking. God is doing his work, either replenishing or destroying things of the earth, so we were to be still.

> *The fear of the Lord is the beginning of wisdom, and knowledge of the holy one is understanding.*
>
> *Proverbs 9:10* (NIV)

When a bright bolt of lightning and earth-trembling thunder struck, it would possess me to run. I would run to the bathroom, lock the door, and crawl under our claw leg bathtub. There I would stay, either until I awoke, or someone took a butter knife and slipped the lock open to the bathroom door out of a need to use the bathroom, or to rescue me.

Why I would leave the shelter and safety of my family, and the solitude of the Word of God, read to me by candle light, I will never know. I was just overtaken by fear. I believe God was trying to train me early on to lie down during times of storm and never leave the shelter of his safety. It seems my flesh was trying to train me as well. My autonomic nervous system would kick in and the fight or flight syndrome would present itself. I always chose flight, not fight. I don't know why, but I was always afraid or scared. Someone would come up to me, and I would run or start to cry, especially if they had a mean look in their eyes and were capable of doing me harm, so my fear level was always high, and my antennas were ever up.

I don't know if this was some type of self-fulfilling prophecy, but because I was always filled with fear and expecting trouble; trouble always found me. This always kept me running to school, from school, and through the gangways, with someone in hot pursuit. I remember, one time a boy was taunting and hitting me and then my friend and next door neighbor, stepped in and said, "Leave him alone!"

"F*** you!" he shouted.

"No, F***you!" and then they were hitting each other.

Oh, was I glad she stepped in! When it appeared she was losing the fight, I mentally calculated that if she lost, he would come and beat me up anyway, so I ran. It turned out she was victorious, but because of my fear, I did not stick around to witness it. I was at home eating a peanut butter and jelly sandwich, watching Speed Racer, when the doorbell rang. The first thing I saw upon opening the door was Renee's fist. She began to pound on me in my own house! She had been left alone in a fight that she was fighting for me. Maybe I would have been better off staying there and fighting my own fight. Now she was victorious in two fights!

Ridicule about my fears never stopped. Perhaps it was due in part to my appearance. I was extremely skinny with big round, bubble eyes. It is no wonder kids began calling me *Bubble Eyes, Frog, Bubbleus Q-Hubbulus, Bug Eyes Slim,* and finally *Bubbles.* Later a woman in the army even called me "Fifty Cent." She said my eyes looked like two fifty-cent pieces. I guess I was the original *50 Cent.* Once again, I do not know if this was a precursor to some type of phobia for me, but it seems I always expected to be picked on by every bully in a half mile radius, and it turned out to be just the case. "As a man thinks in his heart, so he is." I do not know why I could never muster up the courage to stand and fight for myself.

I encountered fear in a different form instilled by my family. It was the fear of white people. I saw it in my parents, my grandparents, and my great grandparents. They would show an extremely exaggerated amount of respect and courtesy when we were in the presence of whites. They would say, "Yes sir," "How can I help you ma'am" while nodding their heads, holding a submissive posture, and absolutely never making eye contact. Now there is nothing wrong with common courtesy, but when it is over exaggerated to the extent that it petrifies you, there is something wrong with that. I never did understand, but there was always an avoidance behavior associated with whites or anything having to do with them. These common courtesies are natural gestures of respect, but in the presence of whites, it seemed that time would stop. Every encounter took my breath, every gesture, every word, as if in slow motion.

My grandparents always gave me explicit instructions regarding whites. "Never put your trust in them, but not all of them are bad. If you find one that is good to you, be loyal to them and keep them on your side. Never talk to one white man about another white man, because you will always be caught in the middle. Never get so comfortable around them that you can just bear your soul because it will come back to haunt you." I have traveled around the world and interacted with men of all colors. I have been let down by all of them at one time or another. I read somewhere in the Bible, "Trust God not man," because man will fail you every time. If we disobeyed any of these forbidden characteristics, when we got home, we would surely be beaten. In retrospect, these actions were a form of post-traumatic stress syndrome caused by slavery. The fear and subsequent behavior passed down from one generation to another, also known as Generational Curses.

My family had been a part of Central Memorial Missionary Baptist Church in Chicago since 1953. My earliest memories of church were of Easter Sunday. We would all be dressed to the "T" in our new clothes, all in the colors of Easter Eggs and paper windmills. It seemed that all the colors were brighter…the pinks, the lavenders, the lime greens, the powder blues, even the whites, as if a touch from Heaven had made them stand out to be more beautiful on that day. I didn't know anything about the Holy Spirit, or what it was called, but I knew on Easter

7

Sunday I felt different. When we went to church we were always on our absolute best behavior, but there was a difference on Easter.

Even in church, that fear factor would always present itself, because people, as you may or may not know, can be so cruel, even in church. That reality made me afraid in church. I had no evil in my heart...I just wanted to play, enjoy life, and have fun. I soon realized there is a social order in church. Even with children there were cliques. When I would try to fit into one of them...well, you know what happened. Someone was always cruel to me or at least, non-accepting. By this time, I was super sensitive to threatening spirits, so I stayed primarily to myself or with my sisters. This prevented me from participating in things such as choir or ushering. I guess by now I had been teased so much that I was reluctant to try relationships. At this point I expected everyone to be cruel, and I often looked for it or anticipated the sting of rejection and ridicule.

I did find my way to join the Boy Scouts of America through our church. It in turn relieved some of the social pressures. We had wonderful leaders in our Boy Scout troop. I then went on to a group called the Explorers, which enhanced my social skills even further. I would like to mention and give kudos and accolades to some of the scout leaders that we had, and I would like to credit them for helping to save our lives: Mr. and Mrs. John Adams, Deacon Nickleson, Mr. Willis, Mr. Vaser, Mr. McKay, Mr. George Crockett, Rev. Huntly Miss Collins, Miss Ward, and Miss Wilson. These are a few of the people who dedicated their time and lives to seeing us through a small, but very crucial time in our lives.

Chapter 2

Learning to Fight

THERE WAS A bully at school named Sam. He was a short, stocky guy. Sam was always mad and ready to fight, forever bullying and picking on anyone in his way. Whether it was slapping someone upside the head or kicking them, it was always something. I remember one day eagerly waiting for lunch; smelling the aroma of food coming up the stairs and into our classroom. The bell rang, the teacher lined us up, and off we went down to the lunch room. It was spam, mashed potatoes and corn day, one of my favorites! I got my tray, grabbed my cookie and choco-late milk at the end of the line, and proceeded to the table to sit with my friends.

Along came Sam. He sat directly in front of me, picked up trash off the floor, and stuck it right into my mashed potatoes. I do not know what came over me, but I slapped him and told him to get up. Although he was built like a bulldog; I stood up for myself and called this boy out to fight. We stood and squared off. He backed me into the corner of the brick walls that surrounded our lunch room. He drew way back to swing, and in my head I heard his fist whistling through the air. I ducked and his fist hit the brick wall, busting his knuckles wide open. Blood splattered and the lunch room broke out into applause. The teachers came and broke up the fight. I was held the victor, but it was not long before the fear set back in.

It was nearing three fifteen, and school would be ending soon. Having to fight, particularly outside the safety of your teachers, on the streets of Chicago was terrifying. It felt like a duel was imminent at the end of the school day, along with the pistols, and counting off the paces. I didn't know what to do. I only knew that Sam, who by now was so furious I could see the smoke coming from his nostrils said, "I am going to kick your ass after school" and there would be no one there to prevent that.

As the bell rang, everyone scurried to leave. I looked out the window and saw everyone crowding around each exit to see which one I would come out of. I don't know what it is about fights in Chicago, but kids always crowd

11

around to see a good one. There was nothing wrong with a good fight, as long as I was not the one fighting!

Frantically, I went down to the basement where the janitors were going into the boiler room. Suddenly I saw an exit that only they used, one I had never seen before. I followed them directly toward this exit, and one of the janitors said to me "Boy, what are you doing down here?" "Sir, please, you have to let me out of this exit, they will beat me up if I go out any of the others. They are all waiting for me!"

"Alright, come on son," and he let me out the rear exit of the school.

To this day, this story is legendary and still spoken of at every reunion. It is one of the highlights and highpoints, resulting in intense laughter, when we all get together. Once again God had provided a path for me when I thought there was no way out. Perhaps I did not explain this in the proceeding chapter, but every time I was chased, it ended with God giving me a narrow escape.

> *I know your deeds. See, I have placed before you an open door that no one can shut. I know that you have little strength, yet you have kept my word and have not denied my name.*
>
> Revelation 3:8 (NIV)

For whatever the reason, God has always provided for me. He has always given me the desires of my heart. Instead of using my fists, I learned to fight back with words. When people called me *Big Eyes* or *Bubble Eyes*, or some other name to describe my outward appearance, I would immediately come back with something snide about their appearance. If someone would say, "Why are your eyes so big?" I would say, "Makes it better to see how ugly your mama is."

I also learned to signify, which is a part of the culture of black youths in America. We used all the ugliness that we saw in ourselves against each other. *Your mother must be on welfare that is why she can't buy you new clothes. You have holes in your shoes. You stink. I walked in your house and the rats tripped me, while the roaches robbed me. Your mama is so ugly she has to sneak up on herself in the mirror. Your mama has hair on her teeth.* I once told a man that his mama had a wooden leg with a kickstand on it. Years later I was at an Eddie Murphy concert and heard him say that same joke and I felt robbed, thinking to myself that I was the one who made that joke up.

I became so good at defending myself with humorous words that people would come get me to have signifying contests with people from other neighborhoods. I was known as the funniest man in our neighborhood, which relieved some of the teasing I received. Sometimes it backfired. I would say something so funny they would cry, then get angry and beat me up anyway. I now realize that signifying, at its core, is merely a form of self-hatred.

Now I use a different form of words, God's words, to hit the mark. That hatred was imposed upon black culture from white society's history of superiority. We merely reflected what had been constantly inflicted upon us. We had been so used to them calling us *nigger, ugly, big nose, big lips, poor, useless,* and *lazy,* that we began to shift it onto each other. If you call your child ugly, stupid and useless, it will only be a matter of time until he or she begins to call his siblings ugly, stupid, and useless. No different than our society as a whole.

All of that oppression and hatred exhibits itself in the outward appearance and condition of the neighborhoods in which we live. In the ghettos or inner cities there is broken glass everywhere. Why would someone take a bottle and just break it on the ground? Sounds like anger to me. It is so unfortunate. Our parents push us to fight back by being intellectually and socially better than everyone else, but they forget to teach us that being better than does not mean being superior.

Chapter 3

God's Provision

MY FIRST EXPERIENCE with God providing for me was when I was a child. At four or five years old, I would wander outside in our front yard on Walnut Street. I would have a desire for toys, for something to play with. As I would dig around in the front yard, which had no grass, I would find to my surprise, toys! I don't know how this all occurred, but I had become very used to the concept of asking, or having a desire for something, and receiving it. Whether it was mercy from a well-deserved whipping, a cancelled examination at school for which I was unprepared, or my favorite meal that I had a desire for. I guess you would say that I had become spoiled by God. I am still spoiled. God gives me the desires of my heart.

In the inner city of Chicago, I looked out and surveyed the hood and its inhabitants. I did not like what I saw, I did not like who I was, I did not like who they were, and I did not like the order of things. I did not like being part of a supposedly inferior race. I began to develop drive and determination. Seeing all the death and destruction; I knew I had to live, I had to have life and life abundantly. Being a product of the ghetto did not mean I had to be ghetto. My deepest spiritual desire was not to be like, or the same, as the people around me, and to get out of the ghetto/hood and God made it so.

It seems like everywhere I went I stood out. In my juvenile state I did not realize that standing out was God's way of setting me apart. It is so ironic that I would ask God to make me special and he did. He set me apart and anointed me. It felt so awkward being alone and different when all I wanted was to be liked and accepted by those that I was asking God to set me apart from. Is that crazy or what? I guess that was God's way of saying you can't have your angel food cake and eat it too!

I made it through the rest of my formative years with no significant damage. I went on to high school and for the first two years; I was a terrible student. I attended the infamous John Marshall High School. If we lost a game we won the fight. I remember walking down the hallway my first week of school; everyone knew we were "freshies, and were throwing pennies at us from every side. There were people standing in the halls with their lockers open; some drinking wine, some shooting dice, some smoking marijuana. Talk about a scary feeling. It was the longest walk to class that I had ever had in my life.

Trying to find my classroom, I had some security knowing that there was a white faculty member walking a few steps ahead of me. I tried to stay as close to him as I could, as he appeared to be trying to make it through the jungle as well. When I finally reached my classroom I said to another student, in the presence of faculty. "Where is the principle, how can they allow all of this, people smoking "rifa" and shooting dice in the hallways? What kind of mess is this?" Laughing, the student and the teacher replied, "That was the principle walking in front of you." I was speechless.

While in High School, I neither studied nor read an entire book. Every time I would begin to read, my mind would begin to wander and dream to other thoughts. My, where did the time go? I didn't realize it then, but I was dealing with attention deficit and bipolar disorder, neither of which I claim now.

I was always inclined to suspension or detention because of my signifying, my "funny man" ways. My way of being accepted was through humor, and boy, did I have humor. I got high on having an audience, whether it was singing, dancing, or telling jokes. Oddly, it was never in the appropriate place such as an auditorium or in a drama class. Just in the middle of the hallway when I should have been heading to class.

In my junior year, I began to run track and was actually pretty good. My track coach, Mr. J. W., begged me to go to college. I told him that I did not have what it takes to go to college. I was too afraid. In fact, I was so afraid I never took the ACT or SAT tests. I wanted to join the military. He insisted that I would want to be an officer and not just an enlisted man. I graduated second from last in my class, but I did graduate.

Chapter 4

The Scheme of Things

I GRADUATED FROM high school in June, enlisted in the Army and was off for boot camp in Fort Jackson, South Carolina on August 8, 1979. What a different world! Here I was a person with an inferiority complex, going into a regimented, structured environment. I was guaranteed to be the last man on the totem pole. I was not the "funny man" anymore, things in the Army just didn't seem all that funny. As a matter of fact, they were downright serious.

My job in the military was to be a radio repairman. It became apparent that I did not like working on radios, so I was given a very hard time by my superiors. I didn't know how to handle being disciplined. I decided to go out and have a few drinks at the military snack bar. While there, I made up my mind to go A.W.O.L. A gentleman, like an angel, came out of nowhere, sat down next to me and asked, "What's wrong brother?" "What are you so depressed about?" I told him the whole story. He then asked me my name and social security number, and told me he would check into my circumstances.

Encouraged, I went back to my company. I continued to be harassed by my superiors because I was not cutting the mustard in electronics. They had me on every dirty detail imaginable; mopping floors, cutting grass, taking out the trash, cleaning the bathrooms, scrubbing floors with a toothbrush, and raking pine cones and branches from a military resort called Clark Hill. Let me tell you, Georgia is full of pine brush. Guess what lives underneath layers and layers of pine brush. SNAKES!!! I hate snakes.

After careful consideration of my circumstances, I decided to save up the money for a plane ticket. I just couldn't take it anymore. I was going to make my great escape on a Friday, to give myself a two-day start before my superiors would notice I was gone.

It was pouring down rain the day of my planned escape. There I stood in formation in all that rain wondering, "What am I doing here?" All of a sudden, "RICHARDSON! front and center!" I broke formation and reported to the commander. He handed me an envelope and said, "I don't know how the hell you did this, but these are your plane tickets and orders for Combat Medic School in San Antonio, Texas. I want you to take these orders, go pack your sh**, and get the hell out of here." I did exactly as he requested. Pronto!

By seven o'clock that evening, I was getting off the plane in sunny, warm, San Antonio. There were women everywhere. All of them smiling, waving, and greeting me with friendly, inviting gestures. Once again, God had provided for my needs. Remember that man I met in the snack bar? He was an angel from God who happened to be a Colonel in the United States Army Training Command. He had the authority to send enlisted men to any school he wanted based upon their entry scores, and I had pretty high entry scores. I guess he wanted me to be a medic in beautiful San Antonio!

There I was in deep in the heart of Texas, home of the Alamo, the River Walk, and Daddy War Bucks: a local disco tech where we would go and dance on the lighted dance floors. What a change from Fort Gordon, Georgia, where the most exciting thing that could happen to a soldier was to be ripped off by a prostitute on Broad Street. San Antonio had two temperatures, hot, and hotter, but it was beautiful. The energy had changed to that of a more carefree environment. I thought to myself, "Hey, I think I can live with this."

On one occasion, some of the guys from my platoon and I went down to the River Walk. After having a few beers, Pina Coladas, and Margaritas with the umbrellas in them, we jumped into the river to cool off. Quickly we were escorted out by San Antonio's finest. We mutually agreed that it would be better in the future to swim in the public pools.

The most memorable person I met while stationed in Texas was a soldier by the name of Steven L. Jones. He was an older gentleman from Joliet, Illinois which was only forty-seven miles from Chicago. We made acquaintances because we were both "home boys." In the military you connect to the people from your home town. I don't know why it's like that. When you are young, you are dying to get away from home, yet the further you get from it, the more you look for things that remind you of it.

Meeting Steven L. Jones was no exception. In his introduction, he always gave his entire name: "Steven L. Jones, pleasure to meet you." He was "prior service" meaning he had been in the military before and decided he wanted back in. This gave him an edge on all us privates because he had been through it all before. Being around him was interesting. He taught me so much about military life, military attitude, and how to take it all in stride. You see, initially I think I might have been a little too uptight; of course the military likes you that way. Steven somehow had a way of saying to me, "Hey, relax. It's is not that serious."

I remember ten of us were sent on a detail to the Quartermaster Laundry facility. There were humongous washers and dryers like you have never seen before. I have always been allergic to everything, and my skin has always been sensitive. Upon arriving at this detail we were separated into pairs to man the washers and dryers. You either put clothes in or took them out. Needless to say, my skin was as itchy as if I was wearing burlap. By lunch, I couldn't take it anymore.

After lunch, we reported back to our assignments where Steven noticed that our commanders had no accountability of us or where we were. He said to me, "Come on Young Hero, and follow me." He always called me "Young Hero" because I was straight-laced, even in spite of the racial conditions in America; I still believed in America, and mom's apple pie. I could do anything while I was in uniform. He then escorted me out the side door.

"We're out of here!"

"Steven L., we are going to get in trouble!"

"No, they never even knew we were there! They never took our names down, plus we all look alike. J"

We proceeded to go to the snack bar, where he talked the lady into giving us a few beers before four o'clock. After we drank our beers, we reported back to our company for our regular five o'clock formation, and guess what? No one ever said a word.

The next adventure I had with Steven L. Jones was on July 4, 1980. The base was empty, everything was closed with nothing to do on the holiday, and Steven says to me, "Come on Young Hero, we are going to have a barbecue."

"How are we going to do that?"

"Just follow me."

We got into a taxi and went to the base commissary. Getting out, Steven L. told the driver to pull over to the side of the building and wait for him with the trunk open. We went inside and grabbed a shopping cart. He filled it with ribs, chicken, and steaks.

After we got most of the items to make a wonderful barbecue, he said to me, "Go back and get in the taxi, grab some bags from the cashier on your way out." I grabbed some bags, went out, and got into the taxi. A few minutes later he came out the side door with the shopping cart. As I remained in the car, he put the items in the bags in the trunk.

When I asked him what he was doing, he simply replied, "I had to go see a man about a dog." Now what that had to do with our situation, I didn't understand. Later, I learned it was something people say in the military when they don't want you to know where they have been, or what they have been doing. Steven L. and I proceeded to the mess hall. He talked one of the KP's into giving us salad, salt and pepper, napkins, and forks. We walked down to Salado Creek Park where we had a barbecue along with a few of the ladies in our platoon. After the initial fear of this obvious violation wore off; I had a wonderful time celebrating the Fourth of July.

Dusk began to set, and we left everything at the site just as it was, meat still on the grill, plates full of food, condiments on the table. We just walked away, back up the hill toward our company. Suddenly, Steven L. said to me, "Stop! You smell that? Look over there. Duck down!" We ducked down, looking out into the mere dark. Coming toward us were two unsuspecting privates who didn't see us hiding in the trees. They were smoking a marijuana joint and walked right past us.

Steven L. whispered, "Follow my lead." He held his wallet out, flashing his identification while saying, "Hold it, Criminal Investigation Division! You are under arrest." These soldiers were stunned and scared. In fact, one of them may have peed himself. We told them to get up against the wall, which was a tree in this case, and searched them. We found more marijuana. We asked them if they wanted to go to jail as this was an obvious violation of the Military Code of Justice. These poor men repeatedly begged us not to take them to jail. Steven L. turned to me and said, "Sergeant, what do you think we should do?"

"We're going to let you go this time," I said. "But if we ever catch you out here doing this again, you're going to jail." Steven L. took the remainder of the marijuana, and I told them to turn and run. They turned around and ran like a bat out of hell.

Steven L. and I sat down by the tree and partook of the hemp that we took from those young men. As we were sitting there, partaking of what seemed to be a sinful plea-sure; I began to experience paranoia, as well as allergies to the hemp. Fear gripped me as I began to think about what would happen if we were caught.

I began to realize that ever since I have thrown in my lot with him it seemed like I had been part of very risky behavior. On one hand, I loved the way that he interacted with people. He never met a stranger. He seemed to know everybody. Even when he didn't know a person, it seemed he had favor with them. On the other hand, his behavior was always outside the lines, and I always liked coloring inside the lines. Even while we studied for difficult medical examinations; he would be drinking beer. Of course I would try and have one, but it would cause my train of thought and concentration level to go down the drain and make me sleepy.

Mostly, this relationship was taking me outside of whom I was, so I decided to limit the amount of time I hung out with him, and made up my mind to go my own way. The way the Lord would have me go.

I later found out that Steven L. Jones was gay. Perhaps that was the reason that he had so much favor with all of these people. At that time in history, before the LGBT liberation, there seemed to be a vast underworld of gays in all levels of life. Undetected by the unsuspecting eye, it was almost like another world or parallel universe, and they called themselves 'the family." This was my eye-opening introduction into the world of homosexuality. I found that they had many other hidden connections that were oblivious to the untrained eye.

I knew since the time of finding toys in the dirt and managing all of the narrow escapes in my youth that I had the gift of discernment. I didn't know what to call this special gift, E.S.P., or heightened awareness. Whatever it was, I had it. My military cadre and superiors also knew. During mock combat exercises, I instinctively knew what to do and what not to. I was always prepared for inspections, even when they were unannounced, and always knew when I was with a losing combat team, and how to pick the victors. I always knew when there was danger or potential danger.

Once, I saved a girl's life during a medical evacuation exercise using helicopters. It was always emphasized to us to never run around the back of the helicopter because of its tail blade. It was spinning at such high RPM's that you could not see the tail rotor. As they were bringing casualties in on stretchers, our medical team was poised to hoist them onto the helicopter. From behind, I felt Private Sturgis leave my presence. I reached back, grabbed her uniform, and pulled her away just in time, preventing her from entering the path of the tail rotor. I never saw her; I felt her. My spirit of discernment knew she would attempt to run around the rear of the helicopter where there would have been certain death.

God's favor has always been upon me. I was once on a survival course where we were not given any food. We had to live off the land for two days. I chose a place to bed down in the dark of night, and in the morning it turned out to be underneath a ripe apricot tree. Glory to God! It was not merely coincidence, it was divine. What a wonderful breakfast!

I was transferred to Fort Huachuca in Sierra Vista, Arizona. Here, I realized that I definitely had spiritual gifts from God. I soon discovered that these gifts must be coupled with anointing and obedience to operate as God determines. One day while at the Post Exchange – it is like a Wal-Mart on a military base- I was browsing through the aisles looking at merchandise. I encountered a young lady and immediately was spiritually drawn to her. I had the strongest sense that we had met before. I introduced myself and asked her if we knew each other from somewhere. She said "No, I don't think I know you." I began to list off all the prior duty stations I had been.

I then told her what her name was and that she had two children. I knew both of their names also. She looked at me in silent astonishment. She then said "I'll be right back."

She returned with three MP's. I was immediately handcuffed and taken to the Military Police Station. There they began to interrogate me. I was asked how I knew this lady, where I knew her from, and how long I had been stalking her.

"I don't know her, and I haven't been stalking her," I replied.

"You're lying! If you don't know her, then how do you know her name and the names of her children?" the sergeant barked.

How was I going to explain this? Because of my immaturity in the gifts of the spirit, I found myself in a serious situation that was becoming increasingly complicated by the second. As I matured in the gifts of the spirit, I learned to speak when God tells me to speak, and to hearken to his instructions. That is essentially what the gifts of the Holy Spirit are, allowing God to speak through you and listening for instructions and direction. When an individual does not utilize the gifts of the Holy Spirit according to God's will, then it backfires and becomes a tool that Satan can use as part of his strategy. Where good is, evil is always present, and light and darkness have nothing in common.

As this story goes, they kept me at the station for the entirety of that weekend. Monday morning, my company commander came down, vouched for me, and signed for my release. Unknown to me, this young lady had been transferred to Fort Huachuca as part of the witness protection program. It seemed that someone was trying to kill her. The irony was that this lady had been transferred from the same duty station where I had been. The MP's said it was impossible for me to not know her with all of this information about her, but God was merciful. I was released and cleared of all speculation regarding this matter after my company commander vouched for me and insisted that I be let go. For a while, they still followed me around in unmarked cars. What I learned from this situation was to always see the scheme of things. Never use God's gifts without His authority and always stay in His presence.

Chapter 5

The Flesh Wants What It Wants

As the deer pants for streams of water, so
my soul pants for you, my God.

Psalms 42:1 *(NIV)*

ALL OF MY life I have been thirsty, but what I received as water did not quench my thirst as I was drinking the wrong type of drink. What I ate for food did not relieve my hunger because I was eating the wrong type of food. It is natural for spiritual emptiness to transform into physical hunger. When you grow up in the ghetto and everything in your life seems to be a reflection thereof, you develop a thirst that is seemingly unquenchable. A thirst for true love, affection, kindness, money or wealth, and a thirst just to be normal like white people. It seemed they had everything.

I recall walking downtown on State Street with my sister, Aleta. I stopped to peer into the plate glass window of a restaurant. I cupped both hands to my eyes to see through the reflection of light, watching a white family eat lunch. It appeared to be a mother, father, and five or six siblings all partaking of a meal on clean white linens with beautiful silverware. The glasses were filled with ice and laid out before them was an assortment of food made to order for each of them. My deprived mind could not help but wonder what it would be like to sit at that table with them. I mentally replaced them with my own family.

Suddenly, I was jolted by the maître d clapping his hands to snap me out of it and then he pushed me, saying "Get out of here, little nigger! You're dirtying up my windows!" I ran to catch up to my sister, who did not realize I had stopped to glance into the window. She was about a block and a half ahead of me and she exclaimed, "I thought I lost you!"

"Letha," I said, "You should have seen all that food they had!"

She began to tell me a story that her friend had shared with her about a smorgasbord.

I said, "A what?"

"A smorgasbord."

"Say it again."

"A smorgasbord."

"How do you spell it?"

She explained that it was like all the food you could imagine in one place, tables and tables of different kinds of food. I said, "You're lyin'!"

"No, I'm not! It is every kind of food you can imagine in one place, and you can eat as much as you want!"

I was silent for the next block as I stared into the abyss; imagining the impact of what she had just told me. My family had never been out to eat: all of our meals had been at home, around our table. I knew those people in that restaurant had to be rich because they took their whole family out to eat. If we ever went to McDonald's, you better believe it wasn't as a family. That treat was exclusive to whichever child was with momma when she went to cash her welfare check at the check cashing place and do a little shopping. Maybe you would get the opportunity to get a twenty-six cent hamburger. On the extremely rare occasion we were all together at McDonald's, two of us would split the fries, and two would split the hamburger. You better believe it was an all-out fight over who got to split that hamburger.

While in the midst of the transcendental meditation induced by the pleasurable thought of a smorgasbord, my mind snapped. Why couldn't I have been at a smorgasbord, eating and laughing? Why couldn't I have more than one hamburger per family? Why didn't we have a car? Why did these people hate us? Why was I a "dirty little nigger?"

These issues caused me to be preoccupied with the things that I was going to have someday. This was not a new thought. When I was a child, playing with my Hot Wheels toy cars, I would say to myself, "I am going to have a car like this one, and this one, and this one." When I saw Michael Jackson or some "hip" person on television, I would say, "I am going to have clothes like that, shoes like that, and a hat just like that." Now I have owned every kind of car that you can imagine, my wardrobe is extensive, and I have shoes that were made in Italy! However, I found out that shoes, clothes, and cars does not a man make.

I felt a deeper sense of pain. I couldn't seem to find anyone who really liked me, or even loved me. I remember one guy used to call me the Corduroy Kid. My mother had found a pair of corduroy shoes on sale. Now corduroy was fine when it was cold outside, but when it was ninety

Now Listen To This

degrees and people were walking around me saying "Isn't it a little hot for those?" I felt ashamed. Between that and being ridiculed about my big eyes, my self-esteem was affected. I had learned to act as if it didn't bother me, but deep down it affected me deeply. As I got older, and even now, I find myself purchasing items, whether it is clothing, cars, or anything else, with the thought, "You won't laugh at me now!"

I believe this is part of the plight of deprivation, or the "plight of the Black Man," because we have never had social-economic equality; lack or the fear of lack, has been passed down generation to generation. We spend all existing money on purchasing things to make it appear that we are not in lack. Do you know how much black women spend on their hair, whether natural or artificial? It is a multi-billion-dollar industry. Bling? Another billion-dollar industry. Now, you do not see white people with bling, artificial hair, or dressed to kill at all times. Normally you see them in jeans and t-shirts, rarely do you find them in formal attire. This cultural curse has been passed down and causes us to stay broke, to stay in lack, always looking for peace through possessions instead of Christ. The fact of the matter is deprivation is deprivation, lack is lack. The fullness of Christ is accessible to all who ask, black or white, rich or poor. God gives generously to all who ask.

> *If any of you lacks wisdom, you should ask God, who gives generously to all without finding fault and it will be given to you.*
>
> James 1:5 (NIV)

> *Now unto him that is able to do exceeding abundantly above all that we ask or think, according to the power that worketh in us.*
>
> Ephesians 3:20 (KJV)

The truth is that the church is lacking in genuine fellowship, love, and interaction between churches. Whether you are Catholic, Methodist, Protestant, Baptist, Evangelical, or Non-Denominational; we are all children of the highest God. We all are servants of Jesus Christ. What is so difficult to understand about that?

> *Just as the Son of man did not come to be served, but to serve, and to give His life a ransom for many.*
>
> Matthew 20:28 (NIV)

Chapter 6

Living in the World

UP UNTIL THIS point, I was still relatively clean. I made it through the wiles of the city for the most part unscathed, and I made it through the constant ridicule of my peers. Bullying is now being brought to the attention of the public, but in my formative years there were no such barriers to block or deal with it. I now know that it was an inherited trait of our culture due to slavery. All of its negative residual particles have been passed down, like anger, and low self-esteem. People who are angry and hurt themselves project rage and pain onto other people. It seemed when I was a child, I was the one they projected it onto because I was meek and afraid. I had the residual particle of insecurity. I was always insecure about who I was or what I could do. I was always asking for a second opinion, a third, and even a fourth.

During my Army years, I was stationed in Germany. Being in the military, in a foreign country, can be a very lonely experience. I was longing for love, companionship, intimacy, you know, umm sex. Working for Uncle Sam sometimes does not permit you to nurture a relationship; so many soldiers marry the first person they sleep with, but not me. I had begun to develop this Playboy, "I won't get attached, I'll just love them and leave them" attitude. This all ended with my trip to the infirmary to get the "silver bullets," ten-thousand milligrams of Penicillin in each hip…. OUCH!

Because of my need for acceptance, I was drawn to a large fraternity; the Masonic order of free masons. We were popular all over Germany, and throughout the world. We wore black tuxedos, bowties, and carried briefcases with our emblems on them. We had several functions and events where there were always lots of women and socializing. We even had a disco train and disco boat ride. I had finally found real brotherhood in a very strong unity overseas. I began to sell hashish, which I got from the Turks, and methamphetamine, which came from a German connection. I got so popular and hip that I bought myself a BMW 740 IL and I drank half a bottle of Remy Martin Cognac a day.

My need for acceptance was finally being fulfilled by the fraternal order. With all of the connections, I became a very worldly man with an ego. I had to have the finest car, the most expensive drinks, and the most enticing women. I had gone from a soldier of the month and quarter, to a soldier who now was leading a double life. I was still a good combat medic and soldier, but I had lost a couple of key components, such as morals and integrity. With the loss of these, I found it harder to be okay with myself.

The cycle of worldly addiction had begun. I would do things to make myself feel better such as increased black marketing, more drug sales, and more sexual excursions. These acts only made me feel worse, so I would have to do something else to make me feel better. I felt like a human gerbil, running on a wheel of sinful worldly pleasures. I wanted to get off, I just couldn't see how to stop; the wheel was spinning too fast. Eventually, the German Polizei, Interpol, and CID were hot on my heels. I made it out of Germany by the skin of my teeth. Thank God, I wasn't a big enough fish for them to chase me across the sea.

When I got back to the United States, everything was different. All the excitement was gone. The soldiers didn't even starch their uniforms anymore. Of all the places in the world that I didn't want to be stationed, I was sent to Fort Polk, Louisiana; the armpit of the Army. Redneck heaven. All of that fraternity status that I had achieved overseas had no influence there. If you were black, jump back!

I dreaded waking up in the morning. By now, I was very knowledgeable of army regulation; I knew military protocol like the back of my hand. It was hard for those rednecks to entrap or discriminate against me with any trumped up charges. That made it worse; they would check and double check everything I did, always on my heels. That is what the Bible says about the Serpent, that he would always be biting at our heels.

> *And I will put enmity between you and the woman, and between your offspring and hers; he will crush your head, and you will strike his heel.*
>
> Genesis 3:15 (NIV)

I am not talking about whites as the serpents, but those who practice hatred. At this juncture I was ready to call it quits with the military. They had passed a new regulation that would have made Fort Polk my permanent home base, and that was not an option. I now had six months left of a six-year hitch.

Christmas was rolling around and it had been six years since I had the opportunity to go home to my family for the holidays. I went to Mississippi and had a wonderful time with my sisters, mother, and my new step-father. My nephew, whom I had always been close to, was now a club owner, living fast and loose. His lifestyle was something I was used to. On New Year's Eve, I went over to his house. His friends were over and everyone was drinking. I noticed a lot of people coming and going. I knew he was a very popular, likeable person, so I didn't pay too much attention to it.

We sat around for about four hours drinking and watching the game. I went into the kitchen where his friends were huddled around in a circle, smoking something from a can. This something was cocaine. My nephew said, "Unc, try this." I took the can and smoked what was in it. I don't know why I didn't say no, I just wasn't thinking about it. I was enjoying the festivities with my family and the holidays. I never gave it another thought.

I had experimented with some things in the past. I had tried marijuana, but was allergic to it. I remember once on Lucy Flowers School grounds, I tried it with my friends when we were about sixteen years old. It gave me the most far out feeling I had ever known. My friends were laughing and pointing at me. Once again, I was the source of their amusement. All of a sudden I couldn't breathe and they had to rush me to the hospital because of my allergies. It seems that I was allergic to marijuana, grass, trees, roots, shellfish, and cats.

I returned to base the following Monday after that holiday weekend. At four-thirty in the morning, I was suddenly awakened by a loud knock on my door, as if the police were trying to gain entrance. When I answered it, it was my platoon sergeant. He said, "Sergeant Richardson, report to the orderly room." I got myself together and went to the orderly room where I discovered that we were having a health and welfare inspection. This is where they bring the dogs through, check every room, and give each man a drug screen.

My platoon sergeant was to retire in a month and I was slated to take over the medical platoon. It was my time and I was ready. I was a highly qualified combat medical NCO. About two months after that "Piss Test" while doing inventory of all the equipment, which was required when one leader is replacing another, I was summoned by a company clerk. He told me the company commander wanted to see me. I reported to the CO's office and was informed, while standing at attention, that I was being charged with having cocaine in my system. I could have fainted. I was in total shock, dismay, and disbelief. I even denied it, but as I stood there numbly; I remembered being in a circle, smoking out of a can, at my nephew's house.

"I'LL be damned." That is all I could say to myself. I was busted from Sergeant to Corporal, with thirty days restricted to the barracks, and thirty days of extra duty. I was also recommended for a bad conduct discharge, possible jail time pending, and no pay for thirty days. What a mess. I was a nervous wreck, ostracized and isolated. Nobody wanted anything to do with me.

I needed to figure out what to do. This company commander was hard and he would cut me no sack, nor would he listen to excuses such as, "It was my first time. I was just experimenting with it." Or, "I was with my family." None of that would save me. Remember, I was in a place where they were not fond of blacks and they did not try to hide it, so I knew he would give me the maximum penalties available and push for jail time in Fort Leavenworth, Kansas.

Here I was coming up on the end of my second six-year tour with three months left. I was also due for re-enlistment and promotion, all while taking over as medical platoon sergeant. Could this be anymore messed up? It was time to head to J.A.G. and get a lawyer. I worried because military lawyers didn't have the greatest reputations. It was always thought that the civilian lawyers were better. I went to see a second lieutenant lawyer, knowing that second lieutenants have a reputation for being "green." True to fashion, as I sat in his office and spoke with him, I thought that he didn't know his butt from a hole in the ground. I knew I was in trouble.

I had come back from Germany and purchased a Fiero GT, candy apple red, decked out with Masonic stickers all over it. When I exited the J.A.G. office, there in the parking lot, my beautiful car was deliberately blocked in by another. Unfortunately, I had parked in the J.A.G. NCO's parking space. I had to go back in the building to see who had my car blocked in. There stood this sharply dressed black Master Sergeant. He looked me right in the eyes and said, "Are you the SOB that parked in my spot?" My soul was crying out, "What now?"

"Yes Sergeant, I am."

"Step into my office."

I was thinking, "Here we go again." He closed his door and walked up very close to me, shook my hand, and hugged me and said, "Hey brother, how are you doin'?" I noticed the handshake was that of another Mason! Now there was a sigh of relief as I literally melted into his embrace. I knew that grip and embrace to be that of a brother who would give his life for me, and I him, according to our Masonic obligation to each other.

"What can I do for you brother?" I told him the whole story. "Come back in a week," he said.

A week went by. I returned to see him and after we greeted each other in the Masonic manner, he informed me of his findings and actions. He first stated that because I had less than sixty days left on this tour of duty it would be impossible to even process the legal charges. He would make sure it would take three to six months to formally charge me, so he informed my company commander that in this case there would be nothing that J.A.G. could do to prosecute me. All that could be done is to allow me to end the tour of duty with an honorable discharge.

I was relieved! I was able to process out of the military with an honorable discharge. There is a God in Heaven and His name is Jehovah Jireh, the God that provides for all of our needs.

I must further add that I have cut ties with the Masonic organization since that time, not because of anything that I had personally experienced with them, clearly God had used them for my benefit, but because as a Pastor I have run into so much opposition about being a part of an organization with alleged connections with Satanic ritual. While I was a member, I never experienced any of the occult or satanic rituals that have been allegedly connected to the Free Masons. In fact, I experienced a greater brotherhood than I have with any Christian brother that I have met to date. However, at this juncture in my Christian life I could not allow anything to hinder me or cause stumbling blocks for others as I minister the Gospel of Jesus Christ, so I cut ties and renounced my affiliation with the organization.

> *To everything there is a season, and a time*
> *to every purpose under heaven:*
>
> *A time to be born, and a time to die; a time*
> *to plant, and a time to pluck up that which*
> *is planted; a time to kill, and a time to heal;*
> *a time to break down, and a time to build*

47

up; a time to weep, and a time to laugh; a time to mourn, and a time to dance; a time to cast away stones, and a time to gather stones together; a time to embrace, and a time to refrain from embracing; a time to get, and a time to lose; a time to keep, and a time to cast away; a time to love, and a time to hate; a time of war, and a time of peace.

Ecclesiastes 3:2-22 *(KJV)*

Chapter 7

Do Not Be Unevenly Yoked

Be ye not unequally yoked together with
unbelievers: for what fellowship hath righ-
teousness with unrighteousness? And what
communion hath light with darkness?

2 Corinthians 6:14 (KJV)

AFTER MY DISCHARGE from the military, I was in a
very quasi state of being as a civilian. All I could remember
was military life. I remember as I walked downtown to
the Veteran's Administration office, counting my cadence.
"Your left, your left, your left right!" It was then that I realized how regimented I was. I wondered to myself, "Is this
what they call shell-shocked?"

The VA placed me on service connected disability for
some of the injuries I sustained while on active duty. That

was a relief because I would now have some income until I found a job. I soon found work at a food warehouse, where a man gave me a broom and told me to sweep. He did not give me a specific area. I looked out over the fifty-thousand square feet of area and wondered, "Where do I sweep?" "Do I sweep it into one pile, or do I sweep it into several piles?"

As I stood there with my chin on the push-broom handle, looking at the vast area of warehouse, it dawned on me. Unlike the military where you were given an order to complete or the consequences would be severe, here I didn't HAVE to do anything. That was the first time in my life that I recognized that I had the power of decision. If I didn't want to do something, I didn't have to do it.

The supervisor walked up to me and said, "Hey man, why ain't you sweepin'?" I just looked at him with my chin still on the tip of the broom handle. Then I just let it go. He and I both stood there watching as the broom stood momentarily by itself. It slowly began to fall, and we watched it until it hit the ground with and echoing "PLAP!" We both looked at the broom as it lay on the ground. I looked at him, he looked at me; we said nothing. I turned and walked out the door.

I got in my little sports car and drove home with a sense of freedom that I had never felt before. I had always been under someone: under my parents, under Uncle Sam, yet here I was my own man, able to make my own decisions. It was a very strange ride home. I chuckled remembering how the broom stood up on its own. I wondered if that man was still standing there looking at it on the floor. It seemed as if we were both hypnotized by the broom, and my act of liberation.

I soon found another job at a medical supply warehouse, working in the shipping and receiving department. I was pulling orders or putting up orders for the local hospitals. I could adapt because I had been trained as a medical NCO in the military, so I knew all the supplies we were shipping. I knew them by name; they knew them by serial number. Soon I was climbing up the ladder of success. Within a years' time I had convinced the owner to start a night shift so we could be even more productive. He made me the night manager. One of the long term employees knew how to play chess, and I loved chess, so we spent quite a bit of time playing while the others were out in the warehouse pulling orders.

I remember the company had a Christmas party at a local hotel. As I was getting dressed, I meticulously put on my burgundy waist cut tuxedo with braids going around the lapel of the jacket; the pants had braids on each side. I had on Florsheim's shoes. I tied my bowtie just right and double checked myself in the mirror. I jumped into my car with the top down and drove to the party. I imagined just how it would be. The employees would be all dressed up and the tree would be lit. People would have their cocktails, the piano would be playing, and there would be dancing and laughter. I envisioned getting out of my car, walking into the shimmering lights all tall, dark, and handsome.

It unfolded just as I imagined it. I pulled up to the Holiday Inn, gave the valet the keys to my car. I gallantly walked in. The Christmas tree was beautifully lit in the lobby and the piano was playing beautiful Christmas music. I asked the door man where the party was for the medical company and I found the suite. I opened the door and there they were. The room was dimly lit with one table in the middle of the floor. There were two kegs of beer sitting next to the table with a stack of disposable cups. All of the employees wore jeans and t-shirts. They were drinking beer and cursing, and it was terribly loud.

It was as if the music stopped when I walked in. They all turned, looked at me, and started to laugh. One of the employees yelled out, "Hey boy, bring me a damn drink!"

Another said, "When you get through with that, go park my f-ing car!" It hadn't occurred to me that with the burgundy tux and the bow tie that I resembled a bellhop at an exclusive hotel, and because I was in the south and I was black I really looked like a bellhop. I had never been so humiliated in my life, but on second thought, I had. Remember the kids on Walnut Street? That sure brought back horrible memories.

I had a couple drinks with them, and lied that I was dressed this way because I was going to a formal gathering afterwards. One of them insisted on continually ridiculing me about my tuxedo, calling me a "doorman," "butler," "House Nigger." Another of them tried to stop him from insulting me and a fight broke out between them. I tried to stop the fight, but one of the white men said, "Nigger, get your F-ing hands off me!" "Get your ass out of here!" It wouldn't have been so bad, but this guy was one of the managers over the entire warehouse.

I left and went somewhere and got drunk. Then I found the 'hood and a broad who had some crack, and that was that. I recall coming home drunk that night. My mother would not allow you to come home after eleven at night, particularly if you were high. I snuck around to the back where my nephew Eric and I shared a room. Now Eric is the son of my sister Aleta and he has autism. He is the sweetest human being I know; he doesn't have a mean bone in his body. Eric is the purest Christian I know. He has never lied, drank or cursed. He just wants you to love him for who he is, autistic traits and all. He would do anything to help you. So I would knock on the window and Eric would jump up and let me in. As I sat on my bed in a drunken stupor, head in hand, full of disgust about my behavior, Eric would say to me, "Let me pray for you. Oh Lord, please give my Uncle Dwayne peace in his mind." It seemed immediately that God gave me prophetic insight. I said, "Eric, I love you. God revealed to me that he is going to give me a church, and you will be my armour bearer."

Then my bills began to fall behind. I didn't have any money, and I was losing my desire to do the things I used to do. I stopped washing and waxing my car; running every morning, going to church, or going to work. I used the Christmas party debacle as an excuse to resign from the company. My drinking and drugging activity increased and I began to find myself in the presence of women that I would never normally be with. I was doing things that I would never normally do.

I concluded that this was a problem and checked into the VA Hospital. There I underwent treatment for drugs and alcohol. I met a patient by the name of Skip Edwards, but he called himself Skip Heron. He used to be a television journalist. I could sit and listen to him talk all day. We shared some laughs as he would tell stories. He had the most incredible vocabulary that I had ever heard from a black man. He could put together a sentence, or speech, the likes of which I had never heard before. Once he said to me, "Dwayne, you are like the village cobbler. You fix everyone's shoes, yet you have the most raggedy shoes in town." I would never forget that.

I left treatment refreshed, a new person, enlightened on addictive behaviors. I moved back to Jackson, Mississippi. I got a job at River Oaks Hospital. It was a white folk's hospital: I seldom saw black patients. It was a very nice hospital that catered to their patients as if it were a resort and not a hospital. There I meet Sara. She was a nurse, very quiet and reserved, in an environment where other nurses were always gossiping and talking about this or that.

Patients would complain to me about her, that she wasn't friendly and didn't talk much. When I spoke to Sara, I felt like she always had to be the cheerful, life of the party; the one who had to set the atmosphere. She always seemed down when she came in to work, and I always felt it was my job to cheer her up. One day I asked her out to the movies, and thus began our relationship.

She had two sons, one seventeen, and the other five. I had a good relationship with both of them. I sponsored her older son's prom, and allowed him to drive my SAAB. He was good and very intelligent. He received a scholarship to Dillard University to study computer science.

Whenever I went to Sara's, there was always a dark cloud over her household. She told me that she had previously been married to a serious drug user. It seemed that I was led to clean up the mess that derived from a drug infested relationship. I was in rescue mode. I was determined to fix it.

Because of my military experience, everything had to be in order. I kept my credit straight, my house clean, my car clean, and I was always a very neat dresser. I was the total opposite of Sara. She seemed to be worn down by the stressors of her prior marriage. At times she seemed hopeless and I could not allow that to happen. The "cobbler" had to fix her shoes. I began to use the money I received for school to help pay her bills. One day I sat her down and told her to list all of her problems on a piece of paper, and we would solve them one by one. By the time we solved all of the things on that list, a whole new list materialized. It seemed to go on, and on. I could never seem to fix the root of the problems. I began to feel drained and used up by this relationship. It was taking me from the carefree, laughing person that I was, to a person preoccupied with someone else's problems. The more I helped, the further I seemed to be from solving them. It was very frustrating.

My sister told me about a job paying a hundred dollars a day, back in Chicago. I decided to leave Sara and return to Chicago where unfortunately, this incredible job never materialized. Another of my sisters helped me land a job counseling at a mental health facility. I enjoyed this job. I was a case worker in my old neighborhood. It gave me comfort to be able to help people fix their problems. I had a case load of sixteen.

I met a woman while I worked there. She was a psychologist, tall, beautiful, and extremely intelligent. We began to date and moved in together on Lakeshore Drive where our views were of Lake Michigan and the downtown skyline; I guess you would call it breathtaking. She taught me a lot about psychology and boundaries.

There was one thing about her that I could not accept, she did not believe in Jesus. She began her education in a Catholic school where she had been hurt. Everyone she encountered in religion was not all they appeared to be. Because of this, she began practicing other religions. She adopted Egyptian and even African beliefs. This never set well with me, none of it. Although through it all we had a nice relationship and a nice home. Things were going well.

One day, unexpectedly, I got a call from my mom. She told me that she thought the son of the woman I used to date, Sara, was killed. I immediately called Sara, sure enough, he had been shot while going into McDonald's while on Spring Break. Some thugs were shooting at each other and caught him in their cross fire. Just like that, her good, very intelligent son was dead.

I went into rescue mode. I told her to come to Chicago and I would take care of her. She took me up on my offer. Now I had a dilemma, living with one woman, getting an apartment for another. I left the psychologist and moved to Lansing, Illinois with Sara. Immediately I knew this was a mistake. I had somehow gotten myself into a mess that I was not morally, or mentally, strong enough to get out of.

How could I tell this woman who had just lost her son and left her home, that she had to go back? What do you think I did? I married her. Typical co-dependent behavior. All of this transpired within a two-month period. I was confused and in pain because I hurt the psychologist, and I couldn't find a way to leave Sara.

When I finally mustered up the courage to tell her that our relationship was not working, she told me that she was pregnant. Now I was truly stuck. As if there wasn't enough turmoil, now another life was added to the equation. I hung on, in misery. Sara smoked constantly, even while pregnant. I loved her, she was a nice person, but she wasn't the love of my life to have and to hold forever. We were simply unevenly yoked.

I began to turn to old behaviors. I visited harlots who either had drugs, or knew how to get them. I never purchased the drugs myself; I always went through the harlots. I began to spiral downward fast and hard. Before I knew it, I was in Hammond, Indiana sleeping in a cardboard box in the dead of winter. There was so much misery associated with the pain I caused that I began to self-destruct. All of this derived from my bad decision making.

This spiraling eventually rendered me back into another facility where I was treated for addiction and other related issues. After being released, I noticed people walking down the street where we lived wearing clothes just like mine. I had acquired a vast array of clothing, some I even had tailor made in other countries, unique to my design.

I wondered if some of the medication they had given me had me tripping because the closer I got to my home, the more people I saw wearing clothes identical to mine.

When I arrived home, the mystery was solved. There, on the front lawn, all of my earthly possessions were piled. People were rummaging through them, holding up jackets as if they were in a department store. My wife and children had been evicted because all of our money funded my last excursion, leaving three months' rent due. Very soon I learned that she had returned to Jackson, Mississippi. I was now officially homeless.

Chapter 8

The Homeless Trail

THE HOMELESS SHELTERS opened at five in the afternoon. There were only so many beds available so I had to be in line early. If I was late I wouldn't have a place to sleep for the night. Luckily, I was able to get a bed. Once inside I discovered every kind of demonic spirit that you could possibly meet. It seems that all of the homeless demons congregated at the shelters at night. There they would tell of their devious exploits of the day. They would laugh about how many victims they had swindled. Every night they knew no sleep for there really is no rest for the wicked. Some would talk all night long. Others would moan and groan. I heard growling, teeth grinding, and people crying. This was their form of rest.

At six in the morning the lights came on and everyone began to stir. We had to leave by seven. Boy was I out of place. The people who ran the shelter knew I shouldn't be there, but there I was. They would sometimes pass out food, but there was never enough. People would flock over it like ants on a fallen piece of banana. If you placed your shoes next to your bunk, they would be taken. I learned by watching others to put my shoes under the posts of my cot.

When we were all put out in the morning, I had no idea what to do, or where to go, so I followed the others. First we went to the bus station from seven to ten. Then as if an alarm went off, everyone got up and went to the library from ten until noon. I now understand why every time I was traveling by bus I would see so many home-less people at the bus stations. I also realized why every time I was in a library; I would see people sitting around looking like they were reading. These people neither had the capacity, nor the inclination to read. They would just sit there holding the first book they came to. The next time you are in a library and you see someone who appears to have neither the capacity, nor the inclination to read, see if they have their backpack with them. You just may be observing someone along the "homeless trail."

At noon we all shuffled toward a local church which served good meals. It took me a few days to get all this down because I tried so hard not to be a part of this group. I went totally in another direction. After two days of not eating, I found myself trailing behind them by about twenty feet learning the "homeless trail."

One Saturday morning they said they were going to a church that served good food for lunch, the Hammond First Assembly of God. I had never seen a church like this, it looked like a huge golf ball. Once inside, I could feel the peace of God. Everyone had taken the place where they were going to sit and a man came out and gave his testimony. In order to get lunch, you had to listen to the sermon. After the message, the women of the church began dishing out meals. When they came to me, the minister asked me, "Do you mind if I speak with you in the back room?" "I will make sure you get a meal."

I went to the back room with him. He told me that God had instructed him to pull me to the side, hear my confession, and pray for me. He said I had a calling on my life. I was different from everyone else on the "homeless trail." He prayed with me. I cried and told him about all of the things that had gotten me to that point. About the woman I could not live with, nor could I send away because of the child. He said to me, "I want you to come to this church every day. You don't have anything else to do." So I did.

At church, people were always stopping me, praying for me, and telling me that God had something in store for my life. I went every day; I vacuumed the floors; washed the windows, cleaned the bathrooms, whatever it took for me to be in the shelter provided by God and to have something to eat. One night a man came into the homeless shelter and told me that the Lord had told him to come get me. God had instructed him to take me out of this shelter and allow me to live with him. He apologized to me because the Lord had told him this days ago, but he had been rebellious. I was incredibly grateful to go with him.

One day he asked me to go to a Promise Keepers meeting with him, and I did. A little old white man with a thin build walked from the front of the room and wound his way through the crowd to me. He said, "The Lord wants you up here." I began to weep because I knew this was the Lord speaking. By the time we reached the front of the banquet hall where we were assembled, the man turned to me and touched me on my head. I fell slain in the spirit. While I was out, I felt the peace of God and I saw the most beautiful light. When I awakened, everyone was dancing three feet off the ground around me, shouting Halleluiah! When I rose to my feet, I was dancing. When things settled down, I was able to look among the people and I could see everyone who had God's peace with them. They all had a glow and a smile. They could see me as well. I could also see everyone who did not have God's peace. One of the men walked up to me with a warm silly grin and said, "Now do you see?" I said, "Yes, now I see"

> *He replied, "Whether he is a sinner or not, I don't know. One thing I do know. I was blind but now I see!"*
>
> John 9:25 (NIV)

Chapter 9

A God of Restoration

NOT LONG AFTER my spiritual awakening, job offers began to roll in. I began working for a steel company briefly until I accepted an offer for a major railroad company. I recall the examination process; one hundred people, all applying for five positions, lined up outside of the Holiday Inn in Riverdale, Illinois. Of the one hundred applicants, only ten were selected to enter the hotel to be interviewed. I was the eleventh person at the door. As the door closed in my face, people began to get into their cars and leave. Determined, I went to the side door through the kitchen, as I made my way back to the lobby, the proctor came up to me and said, "I need one more. Come on." Isn't that like God? I made number eleven.

After eight hours of testing, I was one of the five who were accepted for the position as an engineer trainee. Glory to God! Soon I was on a US Airlines flight to

Cumberland, Maryland. Upon my arrival in Cumberland, training and testing began. The curriculum was set up so that if a candidate did not score at least ninety percent on any of the exams, they would be given a plane ticket back home. Each test consisted of between one hundred and three hundred and fifty questions. Along with the five people from my region, there were twenty-five candidates from other regions of the country. We were all competing for ten positions. After a month of rigorous training and testing, I received the third position. God is so good! Upon completion of the education portion of the engineering program, I was sent on to Fort Wayne, Indiana for on the job training.

I decided, since I was a new creature in Christ and restored by His mercy, that I would give my failed marriage another chance. I went to Jackson, Mississippi and reunited with my estranged wife and children. As it turns out, unevenly yoked, is unevenly yoked. The biggest disappointment in this entire process was that I really wanted a close, loving relationship with my beautiful son. This generational curse has been passed down from one generation to the next in my family. It took many years and great patience for us to get to a place of even footing.

God restored me to a place of sanity. He restored my employment; He restored my soul. In some sense, He restored my failed relationship with my family. After nine years Sara and I eventually got divorced. I was finally able to go through with it. My need for not wanting to hurt anyone had made me hold on for so long that it eventually hurt everyone. At least now we were in the same town and I was able to visit with them, even if it was from across town.

One day, I received a phone call from my sister. Apparently, her friend from church had a message for me. My childhood sweetheart, Brenda Tidwell had been inquiring as to my whereabouts. She wanted to get in contact with me. Brenda and I had attended the same school, the same church, and the same Explorer group. I had always loved her, but there had been barriers to our relationship. I had always been insecure and shy so I could never muster up the words that needed to be said. Maybe more importantly; I had failed to take her to the prom, even after her mother had requested it of me.

I had always been ashamed of our financial situation as a child. Raising five children on welfare, my mother could not afford prom. We could barely scrape enough together for lunch every day. I never told my mom of Mrs. Tidwell's request, I just blew it off. The week before prom, Brenda and her mother began calling to ask about all of the arrangements. Finally, I told my mother and she said,

"Absolutely not. I don't have any money for you to go to the prom." Brenda's family was furious with me! At church they would "mean mug" me, in other words, give me the evil eye. Brenda and I parted ways at that point. She went on to graduate high school with a four-point-oh grade point average and enrolled in an all-white, all girls, Catholic university. I in turn, entered the army.

Twenty-seven years later, she was trying to contact me! I was thrilled to extend my number to her. Brenda told me that she was in a marriage that had gone bad. There was some abuse and she needed my help. As we talked on the phone, I began reading the Bible to her, chapter by chapter, and praying. I leased a room at the Residence Inn for a month and told her that if she absolutely needed to get away, I had a place rented for her, a place she could make a new start. She packed everything she could into garbage bags along with one bicycle for her son, and headed to Fort Wayne. Eventually she divorced and we began the beautiful relationship that I had imagined when we were in the third grade. Now God had fully restored me.

Chapter 10

The Calling

BRENDA AND I eventually married. Like any blended family where each party is coming together with children, there were adjustments. Yes, each child had his own beautiful, unique personality, scars included. Some were more challenging than others, but I love them so much that I can't imagine them having to go through anything unpleasant. Initially I tried to keep them from all pain, harm and discomfort. I asked God to give them wisdom and understanding. May they be protected and kept by the blood of Jesus Christ every day.

Now that we have merged into one family, some of the psychological hardships that divorce can cause began to appear. We found it necessary to try and over compensate in other areas to keep the kids happy, and decrease their anxiety. In other words, we spoiled our children, and to this day, they are still spoiled. We realized we were spending way too much money trying to satisfy an emotion of the flesh that could not be satisfied.

Initially we bought them all cars and paid the insurance and gave them cell phones; this in hope that it would give them a good start. A lot of people would say that is not a good way to raise your kids that they should work for everything that they get. Perhaps they are right. No matter how much I gave to my daughter, she would always be angry about the divorce of her parents. These wounds could only be healed through prayer and time. As we recounted every expenditure; we discovered that most of our money was spent in vain. Reverting back to unevenly yoked, the offspring of an unevenly yoked relationship will also be unevenly yoked.

During this transformation and adjustment period we were filled with the stressors of relocation and changes of employment. I lost touch with my home church and the spiritual nourishment I received from regularly attending worship. Thus some negative behaviors began to creep back in. Some people debate on *once saved, always saved.* I am not one to argue political or religious affiliation or disposition. In other words, I'm not going to debate about scripture, but it is my belief that one can be saved and delivered, yet still choose not to walk in their deliverance.

Here I was, estranged from the ministry that had given me spiritual food, sinking faster every day with money being sucked into the vacuum cleaner of life. I possessed no real money management skills. I always tried to keep enough money to avoid the need for a budget, but the reality is, no matter how much money one has, you still need to budget. I was lacking in good stewardship and had been most of my life. I believe it was the deprivation that affects most of the inner city black culture. I spent so much time trying to get "things" that I never thought about what it takes to use money wisely.

One day Brenda and I were cash strapped and trying to scrape up enough money to gas up the vehicles and get milk and bread. I was so frustrated because we had allowed ourselves to get in this predicament despite all the money that had passed through our hands. We looked in the cabinets and found our old penny stash. There must have been five jars of pennies, and I thought, "Ah, this will do it!" I poured all the pennies into a bag and went down to the local bank around the corner.

Being the new black resident in a predominately white community, I walked in the bank at four thirty. The teller greeted me without as much as a smile. She looked at me as if I were just another brother from the hood. It didn't make matters any better when I placed a shopping bag full of pennies on the counter and said, "I would like to cash these in please." She looked at me and arrogantly stated, "You don't have an account here, so I can't put these pennies in the machine."

"You're saying you can't take my money here? This is a bank isn't it?"

"Okay, take these penny rollers and roll them up." She handed me a stack of penny rollers.

"Lady, this is a shopping bag full of pennies. I can't roll all these up by five o'clock!"

"That is not my problem!" she snapped.

I was so angry; I lost all of my holiness! I felt like just another angry black man in an all-white world! I looked at the clock, it was now four forty. There was no way I could go home and roll all those pennies and get back to the bank by five.

I went home and began to fuss and cuss. I told my wife how I was wronged, all because I was a BLACK MAN! The fact of the matter was living outside of the will of God can make anyone feel out of place, like a "black man" in an all-white world or a "white man" in an all-black world. In this case, it was the unholy choices that I had made that caused self-oppression, not society oppressing me. I felt that I had lost the favor of God.

As my wife and I sat on the bed rolling up all those pennies as fast as we could, there was a television evangelist speaking of tithing and covenant relationships with God. He said that to have a covenant relationship with Christ, you must be a tither, and he used Abraham and Melchizedek as an example.

> *After Abram returned from defeating Kenorlaomer and the kings allied with him, the king of Sodom came out to meet him in the Valley of Shaveh (that is, the King's Valley). Then Melchizedek king of Salem brought out bread and wine. He was priest of God Most High, and he blessed Abram, saying "Blessed be Abram by God Most High, Creator of heaven and earth. And praise be to God Most High, who delivered your enemies into your hand." Then Abram gave him a tenth of everything.*
>
> Genesis 14:17 -20 (NIV)

When we heard this, we looked at each other because we knew what was missing. I said to my wife, "That's it! We are going to start tithing on every dime that we get. The reason we are sitting here counting these pennies is because we have not been tithing." It was as if at that moment, a peace came over me, but nothing compared to the peace that came over me once we actually began to tithe. I felt a part of the Kingdom of Christ.

There was one issue with tithing; we no longer had a church to give to. We asked the Lord if it would be okay if we could bless whoever and whatever we deemed, through prayer, as a worthy cause. Sometimes we would find a Television evangelist, an individual, or a social service program, and we would donate our tithe to them. This didn't go without hiccups. To ensure that our tithe was available, we would buy a money order for ten percent of our income. Initially my wife would take her money orders and spend them on bills or something that needed to be paid around the house. Sometimes she would cash them in when she didn't have money, but our agreement with the Lord was to tithe on our first fruits. We decided to put names on the beneficiaries of the money orders so that she could not spend them. Sometimes we would compete to see who could tithe the most. Our tithing amount would sometimes be three to five-hundred dollars each, every two weeks!

Something began to happen to me; I couldn't stop thinking about the Lord, couldn't stop talking to Him, and couldn't stop hearing from Him. Visions began to flow through me like water. Sometimes I would have a vision and I would be standing there petrified, staring into space. My wife would snap her finger to bring me out of it. These were heavenly visions and premonitions, sometimes far out visions, like me giving the Word to the masses. I sometimes heard heavenly music like I had never heard before, so beautiful that it would make me weep uncontrollably. Once I had a vision of a church painted all-white with heavenly music playing and people lying on the floor, slain in the spirit. A heavenly white mist, like a low level cloud hovering over the people that were lying down, about five feet above the ground.

Once, my wife and I were casually walking when the Holy Spirit fell over me and I started crying. I couldn't stop crying, it wasn't a "boohoo" crying, or tears of pain, it was just tears of joy flowing down my face. I recall my wife looking at me saying "What's wrong with you?" I couldn't even respond to her. When she grabbed my hands, she said she felt the power of the Lord flow through me into her, and she began crying also.

She said "That's the Lord calling you."

All I could do was cry and nod my head "yes."

"You have to answer the call."

"Yes."

Deep down I had known this was imminent. I had a conversation with God years before while I was in one of the many rehabilitation facilities at the VA. While walking along the Mississippi Gulf Coast after jogging for two or three miles, I asked Him, could He, and would He, still use me after all the times I failed Him? Believe me, I was aware that there were many times I had failed Him. As I was conversing with Him, I heard a fish splash back into the water. I said to God, "If that was you responding to my question, show me the fish again." At that moment, I heard two splashes and looked in time to see the ripples in the water from two fish jumping. I still felt as if I needed to SEE the fish doing it. I asked God in true doubting Thomas fashion, "If this is you talking to me, let me SEE it." At that time, as many as ten fish began jumping out of the water simultaneously, like a school of dolphins. I heard *splash, splash, splash, splash*, and I could see them! All of them! I fell to my knees, then on my face, and cried out to God.

Chapter 11

The House of Love

AFTER I RECEIVED the Calling, Brenda and I decided to go to a local "black" church in a neighboring town. When I met the pastor there he said, "You have been called, haven't you?"

"Yes sir."

"I will train you."

He allowed me to preach periodically and taught me how to give communion and benediction. I soon learned that unsuccessful churches have similar characteristics, one of them being negative words regarding their pastor, or church situations and circumstances. Inability to submit to authority is the other. Members began to give me the dirt immediately. He had been arrested for some drug related incident in the past. This never bothered me though, things happen, and who was I to judge?

The pastor and I had similar backgrounds. We began to form a relationship and I told him my history. I didn't go into great detail about it but nevertheless, he knew that we shared some of the same experiences.

God began to open up the floodgates for Brenda and I. True to God's word, when you sow a seed you shall reap a harvest, and reap we did. Around this time, I received a back-payment of one hundred and twenty thousand dollars from the railroad company. I also got a check from the IRS for eight thousand dollars. We began to sow our seeds into this little church we were now attending. This money made it possible to replace the roof and other upgrades that were sorely needed.

Also at this time, my mother's cancer returned, and she was under hospice care. A relative was trying to gain power of attorney over my parent's estate, so I went down to Mississippi to prevent matters from getting out of hand. I went to the state's attorney to legally prevent anyone from gaining control of my parents' estate. After I arranged things legally, I decided to have a drink. This poor decision led to other old behaviors, which caused me to return to my parents' home without my step-father's pride and joy, his car. While under the influence, I allowed someone to drive it to make an alcohol and drug run. They never came back.

My entire family was angry enough to draw blood. This has been one of the greatest regrets of my life. I love my parents and my family deeply and I cried out to the Lord for mercy, forgiveness, and atonement. My family quickly whisked me to the train station, where I boarded a train back to Fort Wayne by way of Chicago before the relatives of my step father, whom I loved also, attempted to do harm to me. This was the straw that broke the camel's back; this was the deciding factor in my truly committing to the Lord.

I find then a law, that, when I would do good,
evil is present with me.

Romans 7:21 (KJV)

This marked the first spiritual warfare encounter with me since beginning our life in service. At church, under the ministry of the primary pastor, what I considered to be miraculous signs began to happen. Just like before, every time I gave the Word of God, the church filled, while the lead pastor preached to many empty seats. No matter what date he gave to me to preach, every pew was filled.

One day, a member of the church who recently moved into the next town over asked if I would come bless and anoint her home. Why she asked me, I didn't understand, though I felt privileged. To be favored enough that someone would find me spiritually mature enough for this feat was quite an honor. We set the date and time. I took my wife and children because our children played together at church. As we drove to the home, the Holy Spirit told me to pray before I went in. When we arrived, I prayed and we all entered. The kids all went into the back room while my wife and I began to pray over the house. I opened my Bible to the book of Psalms, and began to read the Word of God and my wife anointed each room with oil.

As we went from room to room I began to feel light-headed as if I was lifted off my feet and the lights began to flicker. I continued in the Spirit reading the Word of God, almost in a trance like state. The lights continued to flicker, I continued to read, and my wife went on anointing room by room. Suddenly the Spirit was broken when the children ran from the back room laughing and playing. The woman's oldest son who had stayed with us said, "Wow, isn't it strange how the lights keep flickering?" I was under the impression that the house probably had an electrical shortage, but when the young man tapped the light bulb with his finger, there was no flickering.

I became acutely aware of the environment that we were in. We were in the midst of spiritual warfare. At that moment the Holy Spirit overtook me and I began to speak boldly in the Spirit over the woman, the house, and the entire situation until the Lord told me it was complete. As we were driving away, I looked at my wife and kids, "Thank you, Jesus." I anointed my children again and pleaded the blood of Jesus that my family not be affected by any evil spirits.

> *God did extraordinary miracles through Paul so that even handkerchiefs and aprons that had touched him were taken to the sick, and their illnesses were cured and the evil spirits left them. Some Jews who went around driving out evil spirits tried to invoke the name of the Lord Jesus over those who were demon-possessed. They would say, "In the name of the Jesus whom Paul preaches, I command you to come out!" Seven sons of Sceva, a Jewish chief priest, were doing this. One day the evil*

spirit answered them, "Jesus I know, and Paul I know about, but who are you?" Then the man who had the evil spirit jumped on them and overpowered them all. He gave them such a beating that they ran out of the house naked and bleeding. When this became known to the Jews and Greeks living in Ephesus, they were all seized with fear, and the name of the Lord Jesus was held in high honor. Many of those who believed now came and openly confessed what they had done. A number who had practiced sorcery brought their scrolls together and burned them publicly. When they calculated the value of the scrolls, the total came to fifty thousand drachmas. In this way the word of the Lord spread widely and grew in power.

Acts 19: 11-20. (NIV)

Initially, it was a blessing to serve the Lord at this church. It provided an opportunity for my family to learn to serve the Lord. My kids attended church for the first time and also sang in the choir, while my wife assisted in directing. I preached periodically, filling the pews. This became a point of strife between the pastor and me. A wedge formed in our relationship, and soon I was wounded by words he said behind my back. My insecurities and wounded state caused me to fall into some ungodly behavior.

I attempted to just leave the church, but the Lord convicted me to apologize to the pastor, ask for forgiveness, continue my training, and learn to serve in submission. A year or so later while preaching; the Holy Spirit instructed me to lay hands. I began to lay hands and the people began to fall to the floor slain in the Spirit. The preacher and his wife began to try and pick them up saying, "Get up, you will be alright."

It is my understanding that you cannot quench the Holy Spirit. What I mean is this; I had discovered firsthand that the pastor was saying very harsh things about me. While over at another member's house, the pastor called and on speakerphone he began to speak very hurtful things about me to the member. The pastor had similar sin experiences in the area of addictions. When I fell prey to the spirit of addiction, you would think that as a brother in Christ he would have been the first to come and pray with me and hold me accountable through the word of God. Instead he chose to ostracize me and talk about me as if he had never experienced the same thing. Soon God released me from that church and gave me further instructions because the tension and strife had become immense.

I went to the pastor and I thanked him for all that he had done in trying to teach me. I told him that the Lord was calling me to move on. And that was the end of our relationship with that church. There was one problem with leaving; I didn't know where to go. I knew I couldn't be out of the presence of the Lord and out of fellowship. Brenda and I began to have service in our home with two Couples who had previously left the church. One day while worshiping in our home, they said, "Hey, we should start a church! We'll be with you! We can do this if the Lord is in it." Needless to say, four months later they were gone. That was our first encounter with the spirit of inconsistency. Those seeds that had fallen on rocky ground.

The Lord gave us a facility at a youth building in a nearby Ohio town and we began to worship there. We still did not have a name for our church. One day tensions were high at home: the kids were all angry about one thing or another and my wife and I were at each other. There was shouting and no peace in the house; I could feel Satan's presence trying to overtake our home. The phone was ringing... and ringing... and ringing. I snatched up the receiver and shouted "House of Love!" Everyone stopped in their tracks and began to laugh! My whole house, the children, my wife, even I was standing there laughing. I was reminded of the scripture that says, "See things that are not as though they are."

> *As it is written, I have made thee a father of many nations, before him whom he believed, even God, who quickeneth the dead, and calleth those things which be not as though they were.*
>
> Romans 4:170 (KJV)

We knew that was the name of our church from that day on; The House of Love. Since that day, that level of tension and strife has never been in our home again. Just saying the name brings a certain level of joy and love into the atmosphere.

Chapter 12

The Attacks

GOD WAS DEFINITELY with us, The House of Love ministry was His will and not my own. He assured me with several miraculous and supernatural occurrences. After some intensive prayer asking for direction, God again showed me the vision of the church with its sanctuary painted all-white with people slain in the Spirit on the floor and Shakina glory (a divine visitation of the presence or dwelling of the Lord God) covering the place. Then he spoke into my spirit:

> *"Fear thou not, for I am with thee: be not dismayed, for I am thy God: I will strengthen thee: yea, I will help thee: yea, I will uphold thee with the right hand of my righteousness."*
>
> Isaiah 41:10 (KJV)

This verse continued to rain in my spirit. I heard it from the Lord regarding this ministry and also my battles with insecurity; addictive spirits, lust, lying spirits, and perhaps all of things that Adam and Eve attempted to hide with the fig leaf. By no means did I feel equipped to undertake this calling from the Lord without these assurances.

The Lord paved the way for The House of Love, by making it possible for us to rent the youth building where we began to hold services. Our first day there, a Hispanic gentleman walked up with three children in tow. They had no food, no diapers, and his wife had left him. How he knew we were assembling there, I don't know. It was my first sign from God that we were in the right place, at the right time. I told my wife, "Honey, go buy some groceries and some diapers. We have a feeding and healing ministry." Other people began to call for food and other assistance.

The Lord began to strengthen my wife and I through submission; submission to God's Word and to each other via God's instruction. For example, the Lord sent me to purchase two bags of groceries and take them to the low income housing. Without knowing where exactly to take them the Lord directed us to the correct house/apartment. When we arrived inside the apartment, inside the ice box there was a gallon of water and a box of baking soda. The people in the house confessed that it was a miracle that God had sent us with food at that time.

We began to serve food at the church every Sunday at a cost of three to five-hundred dollars per week. This money came out of the account which had the remainder of my railroad and tax money. My wife would look me straight in the eyes and ask, "Are you sure you're hearing from the Lord? The cost is adding up."

I would answer, "Yes, I am."

We also began going to the jails every Monday and Thursday. Sunday in the evening we would go to the nursing home. Thursdays were Christian twelve step groups. We saturated ourselves in working for the Lord. For me it was making new habits to replace old habits. I knew that if I kept myself immersed in doing God's work I would have no time for foolishness.

There were also some signs involving demonic activity that allowed me to know that we were at the right place doing the right thing. Demonic activity began to come against us in an attempt to stop us. For example, when we first started the church, dead animals such as black cats, birds, chickens, and also voodoo dolls, would be left at the front door of our church. People who we became acquainted with in the community began to lie about us. Then during one service, the Holy Spirit spoke to me and told me to bind and rebuke the spirit of witchcraft and incest. Some people popped out of their seats like popcorn and immediately scurried out of the church. One of whom was a woman who my wife considered a friend; she walked right past her as if she didn't know her. I knew then that I was in a heavily fortified area of witchcraft, but there is nothing too hard for God. With him we have authority over sickness, and demons.

> And when he had called unto him his twelve disciples, he gave them power against unclean spirits, to cast them out, and to heal all manner of sickness and all manner of disease.
>
> Matthew 10:1 (KJV)

Later my wife, who had been in the back operating the sound controls, said to me almost in a scolding manner, "Honey, why did all those people get up and leave the church? Did you say something to offend them?"

"No, but God did, He bound and rebuked witchcraft and incest." It was then that I realized that these demons would even try to infiltrate us in order to sabotage us.

I had a member who came up to me every Sunday after service. "You have to come over to my house for dinner sometime. My wife is a caterer, and she is dying to cook for you! People request her to make meals for them all the time."

After about ten months of this my wife says to me, "Honey, he is one of two tithers that we have, and if we don't eventually go by his house for dinner, he is going to be offended."

So I said, "Maybe you're right." I made arraignments to have dinner with him the following Sunday near the holidays. Before going to their home, the Lord gave me instructions to have prayer, some praise and worship, and some scripture reading. I told my wife to bring a CD that was powerful in ushering in the Holy Spirit. We got in the car and headed there. About half-way there, I asked my wife if she remembered the CD. She said, "Oh Honey, I forgot."

I immediately flew into a rage, "WHY CAN'T YOU DO ANYTHING I ASK YOU TO DO? WHY IS IT THAT WHEN IT COMES TO DOING THE LORD'S WORK YOU FORGET EVERYTHING I ASK YOU TO DO? I'M TIRED OF THIS. I'M TRYING TO DO THE LORD'S WORK AND YOU'RE CONSTANTLY WORKING AGAINST ME!"

Immediately I was convicted by the Holy Spirit to pull the car over to the side of the road and beg for my wife's forgiveness. Then we prayed. After doing so I realized that we were about to engage in spiritual warfare. We continued on to our dinner. As we pulled into the driveway, I felt the need to pray again. Pray to bind the strongman.

> *No man can enter into a strong man's house, and spoil his goods, except he will first bind the strong man; and then he will spoil his house.*
>
> Mark 3:27 (KJV)

As we entered their large Victorian style home, there was a Christmas tree at each end of the living room. Sitting on the sofa was a woman making jewelry who was introduced as Aunt Sally. There were three other gentlemen there; one was a member of our church and a close friend of our host. The other two were from another church. After I prayed, our hostess brought out food from the kitchen. One dish was a form of pureed squash with black specks in it; another was white gravy with red specks in it. A seven-layer salad was placed on the table along with ham that was not sliced, but shredded as if it were ripped along the grain. I thought to myself, "Maybe this is what white people call pulled pork."

My wife and I ate the food in modest portions because, frankly, its presentation was not desirable. While eating and talking with the other guests, I heard footsteps. Someone was coming down the stairs. The conversation stopped and all my attention went to the sound of the footsteps. I thought we had already been introduced to all the guests, but I was mistaken. Out of the shadows appeared a woman that I could not take my eyes off of. My spirit was totally focused, and the Lord spoke in my spirit, "NEW MEXICO."

The woman walked around the table and sat in the vacant seat directly across from me, as if pre-planned. She introduced herself to my wife and I, as Holly, the lady who lived upstairs in the attic. The words, "NEW MEXICO." Came to me again along with, "BAD SHAMAN." I asked Holly, "Have you ever been to New Mexico?"

She immediately sprang out of her seat in a rage and shouted, "Who told him that I was in New Mexico!" The host, whom I was considering for Deacon, began stuttering, "I-I-I didn't tell him! I didn't tell him! He is a man of God. God must have told him." At that point I knew that we were in bad company. The Holy Spirit quickened me to speak in the spirit and I couldn't stop. I began pacing back and forth preaching at the same time.

I told them there was only one God, and He is the Alpha and Omega, the King of Kings, and the Lord of Lords. He has all power and Glory. She and those like her will end up locked in the bottomless pit for all eternity! No Weapons formed against us shall prosper!

My wife grabbed my briefcase with my Bible and other things, and we left. On the way out the door, Holly said, "I hope you liked your dinner because I made it!" We prayed as we pulled out of the driveway and my wife threw the black cross earrings she had received from Aunt Sally out the window. Both of us began to feel sick. I had to pull the car over to the side of the road where we both vomited.

> *They shall take up serpents, and if they*
> *drink any deadly thing, it shall not hurt them.*
> *They shall lay hands on the sick, and they*
> *shall recover.*
>
> Mark 16:18 (KJV)

By the time we got home, my wife had recovered, but I remained sick to my stomach, vomiting frequently through the night. For three days following I was not well. Finally, I told my wife to call sister Norine in Chicago.

She was a powerful woman in the Lord who knew how to use God's power much better than I. Sister Norine, via speaker phone, prayed in the spirit, pleading the blood of Jesus Christ to heal me in His name and Glory. Within two hours, I was healed.

Chapter 13

Building the House of Love

WE DISCOVERED that there was a church building uptown that had been vacant for five years. I called the realtor and asked if we could see the building. When we walked in, I was so surprised that I could have fainted. It was the church sanctuary painted all-white that I had seen in the vision! When I told my wife we embraced each other and began to cry. We offered the realtor the full asking price of sixty-thousand dollars. The realtor then informed us that it would take an additional twenty-thousand dollars to purchase the property. I said, "We thought the list price was sixty-thousand?"

She said, "It is eighty-thousand, and I need the money by Friday."

"We will get back with you. We need to have the building inspected."

My wife and I prayed, asking God what to do. We knew very little about real estate and this was certainly out of our area of expertise. In the end, we let the Friday deadline come and pass. Some months later we read in the newspaper that the same building was being offered for forty-thousand dollars. We contacted the realtor and attempted to purchase it again. Like before, we had the money in hand to purchase it out right, but there was another obstacle. This time the realtor told me someone had just purchased it. They were turning it into a music studio. We were terribly disappointed; I knew this was the church God had shown me.

Being unable to buy the building didn't stop us from walking around, claiming it in the name of Jesus Christ. We would circle it like the walls of Jericho as another year passed. We were at the nursing home visiting a woman that the Lord had led us to go and pray over. At the time I was unaware of why we were drawn to this lady. Most of the time she was incoherent and didn't make any sense. One particular Sunday, she looked me right in the eyes and said, "You can go get that church that you want now. It's up for auction." I looked at my wife, and she at me. I asked Brenda, "Did you mention that to her?"

"No, I never mentioned it to her at all."

On the ride home we wondered how she knew about the church. I called an acquaintance who was immersed in real estate and left a message. A few days later he got back with me. "The church you're inquiring about? It just came up for Sheriff's auction today." He wanted to know how I knew the building was coming up for auction. I just laughed and said it was God!

Being in the last days, we have been conditioned to overlook the blessings of God. More and More miraculous signs and wonders are being ignored and dismissed as circumstantial occurrences so I didn't bother to explain further.

I then asked my real estate friend to bid on the building for me at auction. If he were to win the bid I would pay him and he would quick claim the deed over to me. I told him that I thought racism was a factor here. He said that it wasn't, but I was almost certain that it was. By this time, I had difficulties discerning if every obstacle in a white environment was due to race, or was it just an obstacle. Perhaps that is the paranoia of a black man. He asked me to come to the auction with him. I did, but I sat in the very back. The bidding opened at five-thousand dollars. He placed the first bid, and there were no opposing bids. The gavel sounded at five-thousand dollars! Sold! We went to the building, cut the chains from its doors, and inhaled a deep breath of moldy air, but it was our moldy air! Yes, moldy air, all ours!

We went directly to the dollar store where I believe we bought every cleaning supply on the shelf. We called more members to tell them to bring wet-vacs to suck up all the stale water that had infiltrated the basement. Plaster was everywhere. Because the building had set for five years with no maintenance or even heat, the plaster from the ceilings and walls had crumbled to the floor in at least eighty percent of the building. There was a ten-foot hole in the sanctuary ceiling, as well as a hole in the upstairs conference room through which you could see the sky.

My, how different the building looked now that we were the new owners! It didn't seem this bad before, kind of like a used car when you look at it on the lot, you're excited and it looks flawless, but once you sign on the dotted line and take the car home you begin to see the flaws and hear the knocks and pings of the engine.

The other members came with their vacuums, cleaning supplies, and their "Let's get'er done!" attitude. There was just one problem, there was no power! Because of the mold content, we were driven to the outside stairs of the church where we sat with long faces, our heads in our hands. How could all of us have forgotten the one essential element needed to clean the church? ELECTRICITY! Just as despair was beginning to take hold, a van with a ladder on top pulled up to where we were sitting. The passenger window rolled down and the driver said, "Hey, I'm looking for The House of Love Ministries."

I said, "This is The House of Love, right here!"

He said, "I received a work order to turn on the lights next week for this property. I happened to be in town today working on another order and thought I could turn on your electricity today?" Of course we didn't turn this blessing down; we were learning to accept the blessings and miracles as they came. We all began shouting, "PRAISE THE LORD, THANK YOU JESUS, GOD IS GOOD!" all while giving each other high-fives!

On many occasions we would sit on the church stairs, exhausted from the cleaning. One of the local pastors whose church is in close proximity to mine, would walk or ride his bicycle by the church every day without saying a word to us. This would cause my wife to cry and at times exclaim, "Why don't they talk to us, we are Christians and pastors in this community too?" Sometimes in my anguish I would reply, "Don't worry about it honey, they are just rednecks." Soon the Holy Spirit would convict me about that attitude and my wife and I would begin to pray about the situation and for the pastor. This went on for months.

Once I was invited to speak at the local high school baccalaureate luncheon. The title was "putting away childish things," it was a powerful sermon that the Lord had given me and most of the community was there. After the ceremony I began to receive kudos and accolades regarding the message, and I began to get calls from other churches inviting me to speak. One of them being from the church of the pastor that continued to walk and ride by without speaking. When I discovered that it was their church that had asked me to speak, I was filled with joy. Because, one, God had answered our prayers and two, I knew that I was the first black to be behind their pulpit or perhaps in their church. I ran immediately to find this pastor and embrace him and tell him thank you for inviting us to your church and opening the door of fellowship between us because I had been praying for this. And he, standing about three feet taller than me, with a perplexed look on his face, said, ""What? You don't know?" preaching at my church?"

I said, "What, you don't know? I was dumbfounded the whole way home, I couldn't wait to get home and tell my wife. What we didn't realize was that God had gone over his head and touched the board members to call me. It wasn't until after my preaching at their church that a relationship began to form between that the pastor and me, where I discovered that he was maybe not racist, just socially awkward and introverted. My wife had doubts about this because for four years we had been trying to develop a relationship with this particular minister and we could not achieve what we felt was a genuine, holy alliance between two neighboring pastors. A transplanted church sprang up in town and immediately this same pastor had developed a very visible pastoral relationship. Bible studies once per week at the donut shop, and so on. Since then, I have had to pray with this pastor as he was going through a difficult transition of leaving his church. It seems that a vote was taken and the majority of his congregation had wanted him to leave. God had the final word.

I then began to see how, "keeping up with the Jones'" as Christians can be, sometimes it appears as if we are in competition with each other. I first saw this through the story of the bells. When we were cleaning the first floor office we discovered a large machine with tapes in it. We found out that it was a Bell Industries machine for ringing the bells with different songs. So we began to play it, the bells sounded so beautiful and it seemed to be the only thing in this entire church that still worked. Many of us were standing outside looking up at the bell tower, which was hideous at the time. The bells were the most beautiful thing that we had heard and we began to hold hands praising God as we listened to them. As this was happening, a car pulled into a church parking lot across the street; a lady got out and entered that church. After a while she returned to her car and drove off. Suddenly the bells from the church across the street began to resound in a cacophony of bells clashing. It then appeared to me that was perhaps the disposition of the churches in this community.

In the weeks and months to come, we were busy bees, cleaning, hauling, scrubbing, and moving. We must have loaded ten dumpsters to be taken to the landfill. Every room was packed with old, wet, moldy items. One day I received a call from my real estate friend who had aided in the purchase of the building. He asked me to come to his office. As I walked into his office he placed a letter on the table from the Paulding County Court of Common Pleas saying that the sale of the building was being rescinded. My jaw dropped to the floor. I was angry, disgusted, and shocked.

"What does this mean?"

"I don't know. I was waiting on the deed from all the buildings I purchased at the auction. Two of them I received, but not the one for the church, instead I received this letter from the courts."

"See, I told you it was racism."

"I don't know. I would just give it back to them."

"No, I'm not going to give it back. We've done a tremendous amount of work and we spent quite a bit of money on the building already. God showed me this church!" Looking at this in hindsight, I see now that God had it all under control and that no weapons formed against us shall prosper.

> No weapon formed against you shall prosper,
> and every tongue which rises against you
> in judgment you shall condemn. This is the
> heritage of the servants of the Lord, and their
> righteousness is from Me." Says the Lord.
>   Isaiah 54:17 (KJV)

> Trust in the Lord with all your heart and lean
> not on your own understanding.
>   Proverbs 3:5 (NIV)

Every situation that presents opposition from other cultures or races does not constitute racism. Sometimes it's just simply life's opposing forces at work. I was blind but now I see.

> *He replied, "Whether he is a sinner or not, I don't know. One thing I do know, I was blind but now I see!"*
>
> John 9:25 (NIV)

Upon returning to the church I discovered that the utilities were off. We had no water, and this was Easter weekend. I contacted the County Administrator who told me that until the newly discovered back taxes and maintenance fees were paid, the utilities would remain off. I was ready to call Jessie Jackson, Al Sharpton, and the NAACP; anyone who would join in and help me cry out racism!

The Holy Spirit touched me and I simply cried out to God, and He gave me peace in the matter, along with instructions. He told me to go to the house next door and ask her if we could utilize her hose during Sunday service. This neighbor once told me that her grandchildren see angels around the church. She agreed, so first I filled the baptismal fount because the Lord told me there would be baptisms Easter Sunday. I had my son Kenny, who has always been faithful to instruction, to act as an usher at the bathroom, every time someone used the facility, take the inconspicuously hidden hose and re-fill the toilet tanks. That Easter we had eight baptisms. Praise the Lord. God's will be done. We also formed a relationship with our neighbor lady that would soon be valuable to give God glory.

In the next few months I yielded to the court's request, and also to the Holy Spirit, and gave them what they wanted. We paid the newly found taxes as well as the maintenance fees. A few months later we received the deed to the church which sits at 220 North Williams Street, in Paulding, Ohio. Glory to God! My maintenance skills were limited. I knew nothing of carpentry; construction, laying carpet, tile, plumbing, or anything that would be essential for the rebuilding of this church. One day while I was standing in the hallway of the church, looking at the enormity of this project I thought to myself, "How am I going to do this?" A man whom I had seen around town a few times walked in the door. He was one of the few African-Americans I had seen around town. He asked, "Do you have community service around here?"

"Yes, I do. What can you do?"

He went in the bathroom, which had no toilet, just a hole in the floor with scattered tiles all over the room, he said, "I'll be back." He went outside to his truck and came in with wood, a toilet, and other items essential for a bathroom. He took out the entire floor, which had rotted and put down a new floor, installed a toilet, and all the other equipment. Once again, God had shown Himself worthy to be called Jehovah Jireh.

The weather was now getting cold, and in the basement we had a broken furnace. The boiler was completely kaput! I was at the church when my real estate acquaintance came with some of his employees carrying a ten-thousand BTU heater to be placed in the bell tower. Here it was, God had given us our first heater in a building that was beginning to get so cold you could see your breath.

Even with ten-thousand BTUs of heat in the bell tower, God's people were cold during the winter months. One day, one of the sisters in the church said "Maybe I can ask around and find someone who can get another furnace. I'll ask my former pastor. He is always doing stuff like that." In the next week a gentleman came by with a fifty-thousand BTU heater in the back of his truck. His people unloaded the unit into the back of the church. How good is God?

This same Hispanic pastor called me the following week and asked me if I would tend his flock while he attended his mother's funeral in Florida. I thought to myself, "God is moving at light speed here!" Now God was making our ministry multi-cultural. The Holy Spirit placed in me at that time to learn Spanish.

God had shown me several things in my spirit that led me to this church. He showed me the all-white church filled with his Shekinah glory in the midst of the people lying under the Spirit in it. He also showed me different nationalities of people, along with several properties. Different houses, land, and buildings. When I first had that vision, we had nothing, and now as I write this,we have an all-white church not only in paint, but in nationality, along with several properties.

The relationship with the Hispanic pastor was very enlightening. It showed me the different variations of cultural humility. My experience was that white churches have the least humility of all the churches, sometimes displaying arrogance in worship in the form of control. In many instances while speaking at other churches of traditionally white congregations, CHURCH MUST BE ONE

HOUR, NOT ONE SECOND LONGER. What if the Lord had something to say that exceeded the one-hour mark? The messenger would be ridiculed. In some cases, they show very little empathy towards God's hurting people, and in many cases political affiliation takes precedent over Holy affiliation.

Likewise, black churches in their new found freedom from oppression and segregation, have become very commercial in their services. Without the oppression of black people came a loss in the depth of the Holy Spirit during their services. They are placing more emphasis on status with most of the music sounding like hip-hop, rock, or disco funk. Sometimes worship services sound like listening to the radio. On several occasions, I have listened to church songs that did not bear the name God or Jesus once.

Meanwhile on the other side of the world, John Kerry, Secretary of State, declared on March 17, 2016 that the slaughter of Christians in Syria and Lebanon officially met the criteria of genocide according to an article entitled, "Ongoing genocide of Christians in the Middle East," in Townhall Magazine on August 16, 2016. Another article was published in FrontPage Magazine on July 15, 2013 entitled, "Syria, Lebanon, and Christian Genocide." The article states that Christians are being run from their homes, cities, and villages while churches are fire-bombed and priests are being beheaded or kidnapped. Back here in the United States, Christians war with each other regarding who is going to be in charge of what community or program. We are often more concerned with recognition than service.

My sister once sent me a case of Hispanic bibles and pamphlets. I began to pass them out to every Hispanic person I saw. Because of these actions, one night, forced labor migrant workers wound up at my church seeking refuge. As we all prayed at the alter the wailing and crying out to the Lord through prayer, even in a foreign language was the most profound and deepest church service I had ever attended. The cries penetrated my soul. In spite of being forced labor and exploited migrant workers, they still gave God praise. They continued to cry "Gloria a tu santo numbre!" which translated means, "Glory to your holy name!"

It had come to a point in the rebuilding and cleaning phase that I had become physically, spiritually and mentally tired. One night I decided to have a drink. Well you know how that turned out. Bad decision, followed with regret and discouragement. One cold and snowy Sunday morning while trying to warm the church with a salamander heater, my wife and I were in the office while kids were in the sanctuary cleaning, I told my wife, "If we don't have a good turn out today, I am going to try and sell the building and see if we can recoup some of our money." At this point we had invested about $30,000 dollars. My wife responded to me in hurt and disgust, saying, "I hope the Lord hasn't taken his hand off us because of your set back." At that time there was a knock at the door, I thought it was the children. I shouted, "WHAT DO YOU WANT?" There came a reply from the other side of the door, "The Lord sent me to talk to you." I opened the door, and there standing, was a man dressed in house shoes, pajama pants and a wind breaker, he gave his name as Caldwell. There was three feet of snow on the ground. We had seen him periodically during services giving prophetic word to some of the members. But we hadn't seen him in at least two years. He said he was sitting at home watching T.V. and the Lord spoke to him saying, "Get up now and go to the House of Love and tell them that I am with them and I will provide for all their needs. And if you try and quit, you will be like Jonah, spit out on the shore of Nineveh. Again I say, I will provide for all your needs." Caldwell said, "I am going to pray for you and then I am leaving." While he was praying my wife and I were crying like babies. Thanking the Lord for not leaving us. That day at service we had 45 people, Praise The Lord. Since that time we have continued to experience healings, miraculous encounters and blessing that only God could provide.

Another time I was discouraged I told my wife I am too tired to move everything we moved into this building out. As we pulled up to the church there was a gentleman sitting there in the cold with flip-flops and no coat. It was 8 pm and I asked him how long he had been sitting there? He reply since 2 pm." We immediately took him inside to get him warm and my wife went upstairs to look through the new shoes I had purchased on clearance. We found him an eskimo coat. We took him to McDonalds, fed him from the dollar menu and I found some temporary house with another gentleman I help find an apartment. Now this time my source of discouragement is that there was so much construction needed on the church and one crew seemingly had just abandoned us. When I asked this gentleman what he did for a living, he replied, "I am a carpenter." I think God and the secretary from the Presbyterian Church across the street who had done everything she could do for him, had sent him over to us.

God had me assign this gentleman to report to the church every morning where we would do the daily word and pray and have some counseling. He would then begin work in the basement. One day I was feeling very incomplete as if I needed continued prayer. As I prayed I still felt incomplete as if there was something I needed to do for the Lord. Rick the gentleman who was working in the basement, came up and said he needed some supplies. I waited for a period of time, then went to Ace Hardware. I retrieved the supplies needed and walked through the isles shopping. I went the counter, as I was standing there a gentleman walked in the door, looked at me, asked me if I was the pastor from the House of Love. I replied, "Yes I am." He said the Lord sent me to you for healing. I just left your church and you were not there, so I came here to pick up a few things. I said, "Well if the Lord told you that lets go to the church." He followed me to the church. When we got inside he began to take off his clothes. While crying he said he had gone to the emergency room. The doc-tors had given him the wrong medicine and his liver had shut down. The doc-tors told him there was nothing they could do other than give him medication for the symptoms and pray for trans-plant liver. This gave him only so many days to live. The Lord instructed me to get the pure frankincense oil we purchased from Israel. I used it full strength, anointing his entire body from head to toe. While in the mist of anointing him and prayer there was a sound like the popping of the ears. And the Spirit came over me and said, "It is done." Simultaneously he said, "I felt the Lords touch, I am healed." At the time we cried and praised the Lord and thanked him for another hour. The following Sunday this man was in church with doctors reports stating his liver as in full function. There was no jaundice no yellow skin, he was completely healed.

Chapter 14

Used by The Masses

PEOPLE BEGAN TO come to our services and call us on our crisis line like crazy. Everyone's in need of something. I thought to myself, "Oh my Lord, what are the other churches doing for these people?" We began to answer the call and meet the needs of the people as we saw fit. I found myself doing things for the people that other people of God would have frowned upon, but I felt the Lord was telling me to do it. For example, a man who was a chronic alcoholic came down with cancer, and he called for me to come see him at his hospice bed in his home. He asked me to bring him a fifth of Richard's Wild Irish Rose wine, and I did. As I sat there by his bedside, he drank pretty much every drop. I helped him to accept Jesus Christ as his Lord and Savior, to repent of his sins, and I then gave him his last rites. He passed three days later.

A man called me at nine in the evening needing food for his family. By now we had learned to keep our freezer filled with one pound packages of bologna and other lunch meats. We purchased everything that was on clearance sale, and tried to buy damaged goods such as dented cans, in bulk. While in route to his house, he called and asked if I would buy him a pack of cigarettes as well. I could see the smoke coming out of my wife's ears at this bold request. As I stopped at the gas station, my wife said, "I know you're not gonna buy those cigarettes."

"Just let me do God's work, I need to do this." Although this man promised to pay the forty-five dollars back the following week, we did not see him for another two years. He drove by the church on several occasions, but never stopped. One day he appeared at the church, and he apologized for acting as if he didn't know who we were. He insisted on painting all of the trim work on the church. Well, we have a pretty big church, five-thousand square feet, so I went and purchased the paint. The man came with his son and they painted all of the trim work from the gutters on the roof to the basement, anything that could be reached by ladder. I have learned that you can't use God. What Satan uses for evil, God turns to good.

But as for you, you meant evil against
me; but God meant it for good, in order to
bring it about as it is this day, to save many
people alive.

Genesis 50:20 (NASB)

On several other occasions people have come by to receive from the Lord. Food, money, utility bills paid, or gas to get to a certain location. My wife and I were blessed to be able to do it, although some of our holy and righteous brothers and sisters from other churches began to say to me, "Aren't you enabling them?" I didn't rightfully have an answer. I just knew that to whom much had been given, much is required. I was not concerned whether I was being used or not. I knew God was leading me to respond in that fashion, even though my bank account was steadily diminishing.

For everyone to whom much is given, from
him much will be required; and to whom
much has been committed, of him they will
ask the more.

Luke 12:48 (NKJV)

At The House of Love, many people were asking to be baptized. It wasn't long before we had baptized forty-five people. Before the purchase of our building, I had gone to some neighboring churches and asked if I could use their baptismal. I didn't realize how funny acting some church people could be. A local minister had made arrangements for us to use their baptismal, but the baptisms came in so fast that we were using it every week.

Apparently some of his members decided to put a stop to it. One day as I was preparing to baptize a gentleman, I stepped into the water and there the deterrent was: feces. I didn't know what to do. I was shocked. I guess this was that church's way of telling me that they didn't want any blacks in their baptismal, even if the people I was baptizing were white. That church had not had a baptism at their church in years, so I guess that would give rise to envy or strife.

One of the things that were most painful was attacks from Christians. I once had a local minister contact me and after saying, ""Hello", he said, "I just wanted to talk to the fool who purchased the vacant church on Williams Street." I met with him and he told me that he had the money to help rehab the building, and then he showed me a list of everything wrong with the building. There had to be at least thirty things on that list. He further told me that because of the area we were in, I would need a white man with me because I would never be accepted in this community as a black pastor to a church this size. I simply smiled at him and said, "I'm sorry but the Lord hasn't shown me that. Have a good day."

"Well who are you going to get to be your assistant pastor?"

"I think it is going to be a woman." Right before my very eyes, he transformed into a red ball of anger. He did not believe in woman pastors. After quoting me a lot of scriptures that spoke against women pastors he jumped in his truck and sped off.

We moved forward, despite setbacks, difficulties, and attacks. The Lord continued to provide for our every need. All of the flooring in the church was covered with asbestos tile which began to come up. There is a certain way that asbestos must be removed and disposed of. Praise God we were able to remove the tile according to specifications, though it was not cheap. As fall approached we moved right along with receiving God's miracles. A carpet man, who was working for community service, removed the tile and laid beautiful new carpet, which we purchased at a discount. I always felt a good spirit with him, and the Holy Spirit told me to reach out to him.

He was a very nice man, who had mildness in his spirit, but I could feel the connection to evil in the crowd he ran with. Soon afterwards he was locked up in jail. I wrote him letters, and as I look back on it, I know God had larger plans; two of his daughters are typists of this book. Now five other members of his family are also consistent church goers. I guess you could call that a victory, but God wanted a closer relationship with him. There is a difference between being baptized and cleansed of our sins, and being baptized in the Holy Spirit. I believe he was one to be baptized in the Holy Spirit, but perhaps not at this time. You meet a man who lays your carpet, doing community service, minister to him and not only wind up baptizing him, but fourteen members of his family. Yeah, I can see God in that.

Sometimes we become so entrenched in our own issues, in our own walk, that we don't realize what a difference we make in the lives of others while witnessing for Christ. I guess the point is to keep our focus on Christ, that we may see the good in all things that we do for Him. Everything Christ does in our lives has purpose, even the mistakes, even the falls, and even the shortcomings;

they all have purpose. Maybe the worst thing that ever happened in a life could turn out to be the best thing that ever happened. I say this in regards to the carpet man. I pray that his jail sentence be the best thing that ever happened in his life; that this experience brings him to know Christ in a mighty way. It appears God had plans for this entire family to be saved and to be used by God. You never know how, when, or where, God is going to use you.

Two years later, I angrily walked out of a pastoral meeting for what I felt was complacency on the part of my brothers in Christ. I felt so stupid about what I had said in the meeting and at my level of anger all I could do was run to my church, go to the alter and cry out to God for forgiveness for allowing my emotions to take over. While praying, I heard footsteps behind me, and when I was able to come out of the trance of prayer, I looked back and saw the same carpet man I had been trying to minister to from two years earlier. Standing there glowing in the spirit saying, "I just got out of jail, and I asked my ride to bring me from jail to here. Now here I am." We embraced in the spirit of the Lord and I knew that I was supposed to walk out of that meeting because God has purpose in all.

Chapter 15

The Healings

GOD HAS USED The House of Love as a healing ministry, and we have witnessed several miracles in this ministry. There was a man who came in who could not lift his arm over his head. Through the laying of hands, he was able to raise his hands up straight into the air. He could flap them back and forth like a bird. Praise God!

There was a woman who was twice healed. First, she had blood clots in her lungs, called pulmonary embolisms (which only one in three survive). When I went to the hospital to visit her, the Holy Spirit told me to tell her that the following day, when the doctors go to look; they won't be able to find the clots. Sure enough, the next day, the MRIs were not able to find anything. The second occasion, she was diagnosed with cancer of the lungs. The Holy Spirit again told me to lay hands on her. When she went for further testing, there was no cancer.

In another instance, I saw a woman sitting in the back of the church in a wheelchair. She had attended several services in that chair while I was giving the Word. Every week I would avoid her because I was having difficulty with my faith. I didn't feel clean enough due to periods of discouragement. I would fall short in certain areas. What those areas are were irrelevant, because lack of faith; is lack of faith. Sin is sin. It all causes the same results, and those results are ineffectiveness in operating in the power of God. So every week I would see this woman, as if God were taunting me, "Here I am standing at the door knocking, come and utilize my power. Let me use you."

> Here I am! I stand at the door and knock. If anyone hears my voice and opens the door, I will come in and eat with that person, and they with me.
>
> Revelations 3:20 *(NIV)*

Every Sunday during my time of discouragement; I would beg God for forgiveness. I would cry out to him for repentance of my sin and weakness. With this matter the Holy Spirit instructed me to fast and pray, and I was obedient to his word. The following Sunday, here was the lady in the wheelchair; He sent her again. I know God was sending her because our church was not currently wheelchair accessible. As I was preaching, I was thinking to myself, "How is she getting in here?"

God was still yet shaping me, molding me, maturing me. Oh, and that blessed day I finally allowed him to use me! I was filled with his Glory in the Holy Spirit and I called her out. Glory to God. I said to her, "In the name of Jesus Christ, I command you to walk to me now!" She trembled as she stood up out of her chair and walked on her clubbed feet. Step by step, she walked all the way down the aisle to me. I laid hands on her and anointed her!

The church began to praise God and shout. I thanked God inwardly because I felt that the surrounding community was trying to renounce the fact that the Spirit filled our church. There were several members of our church attending some classes on healing, sponsored by another minister. I had difficulty with this because I believe that only God gives the power and authority to heal in His name.

And when he had called unto him his twelve disciples, he gave them power against

unclean spirits, to cast them out, and to
heal all manner of sickness and all manner
of disease.

Matthew 10:1 (KJV)

The following week, that same young lady walked down the aisle to be married. All Glory to God!

Another miracle occurred concerning a young man whose mother I had met two years' prior in a Dollar General Store. She asked me then to pray for her son, and we prayed in the aisles for him. By then, God had taught me to pray right where I stood and not to tell anyone that I would pray for them later, or when I got home.

Two years later the son came to church with her. Despite having tattoos and piercings from head to toe, he was a very non-threatening person who spoke softly with a form of humility. One thing I noticed about him was that he was jaundiced. He continued to come to church, and I could see that he was attentive to the word but something was still holding him back from surrendering to Christ. Finally, one day he surrendered to the Lord and he was baptized. He gave his life over to the Lord. Not only was he baptized, but his seven children and also his father were baptized as well in the Spirit. Isn't that awesome?

After several weeks he confessed that he was on the liver transplant list. He had developed liver cancer and cirrhosis of the liver from years of drinking and hard-core drug use, although he was only thirty-six years old. In the midst of a sermon the Holy Spirit spoke to me and had me speak healing into three peoples' lives. They were all either waiting on lab results, or transplants. I said to them, "Thus says the Lord, when they go to find your cancers, it will not be there." Monday morning at seven, I received a call from the individual who was to receive the liver transplant. He told me that the doctors had prepped him for surgery, sedated him, and were taking him down for the transplant, when the final MRI's and scans revealed to them that there was no cancer and no cirrhosis to be found. They canceled the surgery and he was home by Monday evening. Praise be to God!

Brenda I lived. Our neighbor is the is a few miles from town. Our neighbor is the type of person who would do anything for you if he could. He walks around shirtless all summer long, beer can in his hand, and using language you would not believe. Every other word is a curse word. If I ever needed help in the garden, he would till it. I had a tree fall in my yard, and he cut it all up and stacked the firewood. He was a kind man, even if he was rough around the edges.

Once we had some "church folk" over to the house for a little barbeque dinner. Now, hospitality, "diaconal," in the Greek, is one of my gifts and in this case, I was being extra hospitable because we needed all of the tithers we could get. These people were financially secure and had shown themselves to be good tithers. While we were sitting at the outdoor table, my neighbor leaned over the fence and began his neighborly monologue. Curse this, and curse that. My guests were cringing, as was I to some degree. When he came around the fence with a beer can in his pocket, one can in his hand, and sat at the table, I noticed that a couple of my guests began to ready themselves to leave.

I was almost ready to send him back to his own yard when the Holy Spirit spoke to me. I was to offer him something to eat. My guests frowned upon this and got up to leave. At that time, I was faced with a decision to send my neighbor away or to give into the snarling condemnation from my members who I discovered had an attitude of self-righteousness and superiority. Well, I let the members leave because Jesus came for the sick and not the well, the well need no physician. So we sat there laughing and talking when I began to speak the Word of God. I invited him to come to church. He looked me right in the eyes and said, "If you ever see me in a church, it will be in a casket." Wow, that was deep.

One day I needed help at the church. A leak had developed upstairs and my neighbor volunteered to come and help fix it. While we were standing upstairs, overlooking the balcony, his focus was on the altar. One minute led to two, and then tears began to roll down his face.

I put one arm around his shoulder and I began to pray with him the sinners' prayer. I asked him if he would accept Jesus as his Lord and Savior. He said he would, but didn't know how much he would come to church. He asked me to please forgive his tears, but the last time he was in this church; his father was downstairs in a casket. I never knew that this was the church where his father's funeral had been held. I later learned that his mother was killed breaking up a fight in the bar that his parents owned. I realized that you never know what causes a person's heart to harden, but I feel that it is our job to always display patience and love.

Love never fails.

1 Corinthians 13:8 *(*NIV)

One day, a couple of years after this encounter with my neighbor, as we returned home from church; my wife and I noticed two people standing back beyond our garage on another portion of our property. "Who is that?" my wife asked. As they began to walk towards our car, we realized that it was my neighbor's wife who had been recently diagnosed with lung cancer and had one of her lungs removed, accompanied by their granddaughter. His wife was very thin. As they approached the car, my wife and I got out and gave her a hug. She said that the Lord told her to come over to us, so here she was. I told her to come into the house and asked my wife to get the oil she carried readily in her purse.

We were already filled with the Spirit; and our house is always anointed with the peace of God. When the granddaughter walked into our home, tears began to flow. My wife and I began to pray, and the Holy Spirit began to work. Once again, the Holy Spirit told me to speak to her and tell her she was healed. I saw her three months later, she stopped me and said, "Guess what! I am cancer free, I am healed." We gave God praise and the glory right there. Now I would have loved for this family to join us in church one time, but it never happened. That did not stop God from allowing us to minister into their lives as neighbors. This was literally a case of loving thy neighbor as thyself.

One young man, who had been baptized along with his entire family, was being pursued by the one who kills, steals, and destroys. All eighteen members of his family had been overshadowed by the negativity and the lack of joy that accompanied that spirit. More than that, an anxiety caused the majority of them to have an intense relationship with cigarettes, believing they needed them in order to calm them down. They never saw that the tobacco never calmed them down.

The evil spirit attempted to isolate and alienate this young man through separation. When it first came to my attention; I was driving down the street on a cold, snowy day. There must have been a foot of snow on the ground. In the distance, under a picnic shelter, sitting in the cold, I could see a young man. I said to myself, "That's the young man that I saw out walking earlier." I had a strong desire to go over to him and minister to him. What I mean by ministering to him was this, "Hey brother, how you doin'? Are you okay? Do you need to talk? The Lord sent me here to ask you that."

I only had five or ten minutes until service started and I was on my way to purchase salt for the stairs, so I didn't talk to him. The entire time I was at the store, I was downcast because I didn't get the opportunity to go over and minister to him. I felt that the Lord was urging me to because I had seen him twice that day. Instead, I returned to the church and salted the stairs so people would not be confronted with a slipping hazard.

Now the service began. The praise and worship band was jamming for the Lord, and people were worshiping. As I made my way up to the podium, I looked out over the people, and my soul was immediately lifted. There, sitting in the front row was the young man. Now the Lord began to pour out of me prophetic words regarding him, and this word was binding, was breaking, was blocking, and loosening all at the same time. Now I have even greater clarity on God's Word that says,

> *But God demonstrates his own love for us*
> *in this; While we were still sinners, Christ*
> *died for us.*
>
> Romans 5:8 (NIV)

God had prepared this sermon a week earlier for him. Through that sermon; God spoke the words that broke his depression, broke his suicidal thoughts, and his anguish over a failed relationship. Not only that, but he came up to the front and received healing from a physical injury. Now God's work was completed; he received an emotional and a physical healing.

One February morning as I peeked out of the curtains, the landscape was blanketed with a foot and a half of fresh, white snow. Nothing made a sound and the peace of God was surreal. As I stood there staring, thanking God for allowing me to see His beauty in winter solace; I heard the announcement over the local television station that the state highway patrol had put up a level three travel advisory and only necessary personnel were allowed on the roads. At that moment only two things were on my mind. One was coffee, bacon, and eggs which we had none of. The other was checking on the church to ensure that no pipes had frozen, and that the sidewalks needed shoveled before it turned to ice. I told my wife, "C'mon Honey, we gotta go to the church. After we check it out, I'm going to pick up some eggs, bacon, and coffee, and then when we get home I will make us a wonderful break-fast." As Honey reluctantly put on her boots, coat, hat, and gloves, she said, "Yes, we do need some coffee, and a nice breakfast sure sounds good."

At this juncture in our spiritual walk, it was becoming clear to me that my zeal for the new church, all the repairs to an eighty-year old building, and the new ministry, had exacerbated my wife and children. I felt that the breakfast portion was the only one to register with my wife. At this point, God was placing on me a lot of what I call "Abram" moves. "Just get up and go. I'll tell you where you're going once you start moving."

> The Lord said to Abram, "Go from your country, your people, and your father's household to the land I will show you.
>
> Genesis 12 (NIV)

My wife was not so receptive to the "Abram" moves. It was always; "Why we gotta go here? Why we gotta go there? We've been driving all day; can't we just go home? Can't we pray for them tomorrow? I'm tired, I just got off work." Needless to say that after we had checked the church and picked up the bacon, eggs, and coffee, she was verbally expressing her dislike of riding around. The side of my head began to burn from her piercing laser vision, as she stared at the side of my head.

Finally, she sighed, "Why are we driving around?"

"Okay, okay, we're gonna go home now, but let's go this way." As we drove, we saw what appeared to be flashing taillights in the air. As we got closer, we realized that it was a vehicle that had run off the road into the ditch. The ditch was about fifteen feet deep, filled with water covered with ice. I pulled my car over to the side and as I inched as close as I could to the vehicle; I could see it was pointed nose down in the ditch, submerged in water up to the front door. I slid my way down to the rear doors and opened one of them and peered in.

Staring back at me were two sets of beautiful blue eyes, one of a lady in shock and one of an infant that the lady was holding in her arms above the water, which was up to her chest. Neither of them was crying, they just stared at me. I said, "Hi, you're gonna be alright. The Lord sent me here." The woman cried out, "Thank you Jesus!" and I said to her, "Hand me the child." She didn't respond, so I said to her again, "Hand me the baby, it's okay." Finally, she handed me the child. I guess she was momentarily taken aback that this angel was black. I handed the child to my wife, and she put the baby into our car where it was warm.

By this time, another passer-by had come to assist me, and we began to maneuver the woman out of the car, so as not to cause it to shift. We finally got her out, and into our vehicle where we waited for the tow truck and an ambulance. Thirty minutes later, we saw lights flashing. I said to my wife, "Here come the PoPo!" and the baby said, "PoPo!" We all started laughing because the baby would not stop saying "PoPo!" The mother said that the child had just begun to speak, so I guess I can be attributed to the baby's first words spoken in Ebonics. My wife apologized to me, "I'm sorry that I got impatient with you. I'm learning now that the Lord speaks to you and sends you on assignments. I will be more submissive and cognizant of that in the future." I replied, "I love you too, baby."

Chapter 16

Wild Bill

WILD BILL IS my brother-in-law, and the first true love of my sister's life. I know my sister, and I know when she is head over heels for something, or someone. I also know when she is into something, she is in it two-hundred percent. When she took a notion to do something as a child, she generally did it until it was overdone. When she got into second grade she read so hard and learned so fast that she skipped a grade. She skipped three grades in her life, graduating three years early. When she decided to save money, she saved money. She still has the quarters that my grandfather gave her when she was a child.

My sister is actually, in my opinion, a genius. Now her heart told her to make an investment in Bill. I have never seen two people more in love. As I met, and examined him (not that I judge, but it is a brother's right to examine),

I fell in love with him myself. He is funny, straight-forward, and if he feels there has been some wrong-doing pertaining to my sister; he will give you a call to clarify your intentions. One year after they were married, he was diagnosed with rectal cancer. My sister came to me with tears rolling down her face, and if you ever see my sister's tears, they are bigger than most. She has big crocodile tears. Oh how my heart sank. I could see the fear trying to overcome her, so I immediately went into intercession.

> *Therefore confess your sins to each other and pray for each other so that you may be healed. The prayer of a righteous person is powerful and effective.*
>
> James 5:16 (NIV)

The doctors had given Bill six months to live, but that was six years ago. Yes, the effectual fervent prayer of a righteous man avails much! Recently, I called my sister and said, "Now you know I've got to come down and see Bill." "When do you plan on coming down to see him?" She replied as if to say, "How much time do you think he has? So if you are coming, come." I had been putting this visit off for some years. Every time I thought I'd get an opportunity to go see Bill and my sister, an issue came up around the church, such as a leaky roof, broken pipe, or some other urgent matter that needed repair. This eighty-year-old building seems to always need repairs. It always seemed to eat up my vacation fund, or money set aside for personal use.

I remembered that Bill was a wonderful chess player. We enjoyed sitting around playing chess, listening to jazz, and talking. He was a worthy opponent, and to my dismay; he usually beat me. I think that my defeat could be attributed to the wonderful jokes and stories he told. During one of our chess matches, he told me that while driving through Valdosta, Georgia, the police had stopped him for speeding. Not only did they give him a ticket, but they impounded his vehicle, and put him on a work farm to work until further notice. Bill said that when they found out that he was an electrician, they put him to work in a hospital under construction in the town. He had to return to his holding house to sleep at night.

After a month of working there, the judge finally decided that his fine was paid and he was going to release him. Some of the other inmates, who were all black and of rural decent, had been working there for years. There was an uproar when they found out Bill was being released. Bill said he could see the judge's car coming down a dirt road, kicking up dust everywhere. The judge slammed on the brakes and slid into the parking lot sideways. When the judge got out of the car and the dust cleared, he said, "Now wait just a darn blain minute here. What's this I hear about ya'll trying to go against me? Don't I give you all the pecans you can eat?" Bill said the uproar immediately simmered down to a whisper and one of the men said, "Yessum, you do give us all the pecans we can eat."

The judge replied, "So what's this I hear about you boys tryin' to leave and go against me?"

Now if this story took place in the nineteen-twenties or thirties it may have been feasible, but this was the new millennium. My wife and I have a running joke when one of us feels we have had just about all we can take of each other, we simply look at the other and say "Honey, don't I give you all the pecans you can eat?" Then we laugh. Now you can see why Bill beat me so much in chess, he distracted me with his fascinating stories (or cryptic lies). Later, I learned that this story was true.

After the conversation with my sister; I decided to drive down to Alabama and see them. On my way, the Lord placed in my spirit a longing to pray for my brother-in-law like I never had before. We generally say that we will pray for someone, but how deep, how long, and how often do we actually pray for them? The Lord placed in my spirit at that moment to go as deep as I could in intercessory prayer. I literally prayed the entire twelve-hour drive, only stopping for gas, food, or to listen to the radio for a short while. My main state of mind was speaking to God through prayer. Thanking God for all he had done for me, every little detail, begging him for forgiveness for my faults and failures, and begging for Bill's life.

When I arrived, I entered a home that was battle-weary. My sister was stressed, and very detail-oriented to infection control, dressing changes, diet, and medication regiment, to the point she was nerve-wrecked and repetitive. Bill was receiving antibiotics twice a day via IV, along with nephrostomy tubes coming from each kidney, a colostomy bag, and a port in his chest. He was bed-ridden and in extreme pain.

As I have learned, every time I want to do the Lord's work, or attempt to get into his presence; Satan attempts to interrupt me. Now I have severe allergies to pets and just about everything. Everywhere that I would sit, the dogs were on me. When I would try to get into the spirit to lay hands on Bill and Robin, the dogs would interrupt me. I was almost ready to turn around and leave, but the Holy Spirit quickened me to get into my room and pray.

I showered and returned to my room, where I began to pray, binding the strongman.

> *No man can enter into a strong man's house, and spoil his goods, except he will first bind the strong man; and then he will spoil his house.*
>
> Mark 3:27 (KJV)

The bed at their house was the most uncomfortable bed I had ever slept in, but the Lord made it all right. I slept across it sideways. By the next morning, the Lord had strengthened me and had given me focus. I got up, made coffee, made breakfast, and immersed myself in the nursing care needs of Bill. I felt like a combat medic again, irrigating tubes, changing dressings, emptying bags, sanitizing equipment, and assessing the status of the patient. During every break I would read the Word to Bill. I anointed the house from front to back and prayed often with him. The first day, he stayed in bed. The second day, he desired to get up and sit in his recliner. My sister had taken the dogs over to her friend's house due to my severe allergies. I turned the TV on and attempted to stay on the Christian channel, but mostly we continued to view what he wanted to watch. With every opportunity, I would take his hand or lay hands on him and pray with him.

Again, truly I tell you that if two of you on earth agree about anything they ask for, it will be done for them by my Father in Heaven.

Matthew 18:19 (NIV)

The third day, the same routine, only this time I decided to go out to get something to eat. I picked up Burger King breakfast sandwiches and Crispy Cream donuts, coffee, and juice. The Burger King sparked his interest. He ate it, but immediately vomited. The following day, same routine, more prayer, more anointing; the Holy Spirit was in the house. Also, more food. I got Burger King, McDonald's, and also soul food like fried chicken, fried livers, macaroni and cheese, and collard greens; all from a local soul food restaurant. Well on this day, the livers and macaroni and cheese peaked his interest, so he ate some.

I had been praying that the Lord would give him an appetite, and he was prescribed medical marijuana for that purpose, but my sister said he would have bad trips off from it, and boy could I relate to that! Instead of letting it go to waste, I think that every now and then she would take a few puffs to calm her nerves. Sometimes she would come out of the back room with this far out look on her face. On day five, I made breakfast. French toast, eggs, bacon, and grits; Bill ate every bit of it. While we were eating, he said that there was a place in New York that had the best hot dogs. We reminisced about him having a hot dog stand when he lived in New York. I could relate because I had started a barbeque stand to help with the costs of The House of Love Ministry. We talked about how we loved to be vendors at state fairs. He said, "Hey, at Sam's Club they have good hot dogs, almost like New York. Can we go there for lunch?"

"Sure!" With little assistance I got him into the car and after his appointment with his Oncologist, we drove to Sam's Club to get hot dogs. We had a foot long, all beef, jumbo hot dog with chili, cheese and onions, and we ate it all. We made it all the way home and Bill kept it down.

The following day I made French toast again, since it was a hit, and bacon, eggs, and Burger King. Again, he ate all of it. For lunch we went by the soul food restaurant and I had chicken, but all he ate was a salad. When we got home he said to me, "You know what I have a taste for? Pork chops." So my sister and I went and bought one-inch thick pork chops. I marinated them and fried them with rice, gravy, string beans, and rolls. He ate it all.

We prayed that night. I laid hands, and anointed him. I called for healing by the power of Jesus Christ. The Holy Spirit informed me that when He heals him, he must give God the glory, go to church, and actively participate. By this time Bill was up walking around, eating food, and so the Holy Spirit told me that the following day I would leave. We had an extensive prayer the night before, and then we all went to bed. The next morning, I woke to the smell of eggs, bacon, and coffee that *Bill* had made for *me!* Isn't God good? Bill had regained his strength. When I had been on the road for about five hours, I called my sister and asked her how everything was going. She said that Bill left just after I did, on his motorcycle, and had not returned yet. He had gone riding with his motorcycle friends. Mission accomplished!

The Lord has since taken Bill home. God allowed me to see a portion of Bills transition into Heaven. I must inform you that they have motorcycles in Heaven like you've never seen before. The engines sound like thunder, and Jesus has the coolest bike of all. Now Bill rides with a group called the disciples, accompanied by twelve tribes. The last time I saw him, they were riding about 144,000 deep.

Chapter 17

The Bluegrass Band

WE WERE SPENDING money at such an alarming rate to operate The House of Love Ministries that a decision was made to raise money by selling hot dogs and barbeque under a tent in front of the church. I had always dreamed of owning my own concession stand, whether selling hot dogs or snow cones. I had always admired the vendors in Chicago. I also remember the Good Humor man in his white uniform and hat. I always thought that they were so cool, plus, they always brought smiles to the people's faces.

One day while at the Paulding County Fair, we were selling barbeque from a very small grill under a tent with a few roasters. A man walked up to me and said, "Would you be interested in buying a concession stand? I've got one at a really good price." Wouldn't you know it, another miracle from God. The man had a 10' x 20', fully equipped stand ready to roll. I always dreamed of having one, selling hot dogs and ice cream, but now God made it so. We purchased it in order to have a means of making money for the church. Soon after, as I was driving my father-in-law to the train station, on the side of the road was a huge smoker on wheels for sale. It was so big you could put a hundred chickens in it at one time, and the owner was asking the right price. Once again, God provided for us. In this case, He was our Jehovah Jireh, the God who provides for all our needs.

Things were falling into place at The House of Love. We were making repairs; stopping leaks, painting walls, and seeing people come in. We were missing one thing, we still had no music. We prayed for a singer, a piano player, or a worship band. Once while we had our barbeque stand at a bluegrass festival, there was a little girl who caught my attention. She looked frail and hungry. I was there barbequing and smoking the meats when the Holy Spirit spoke to me, "Feed her." I reached out to her saying, "I need a taste tester. Would you be my taste tester today?" Her face lit up. She said, "Yea, sure!" I gave her a nice sample of the ribs, coleslaw, and baked beans.

She went away with the food, and it wasn't very long until she came back with others who looked like they could use a meal as well. Trying to be respectful of their situation, I told them I needed more *taste testers*. One man stood six-foot tall, and maybe weighed three-hundred pounds; I needed a bigger sample for him and God provided. My wife scolded me for giving too much food away, but I told her we live by kingdom principles, what a man soweth, he also shall reap.

Wouldn't you know it, I went into the bluegrass barn where the bands were playing, and a new band had just taken the stage. I heard a little itty-bitty girl's voice say, "We want to dedicate this song to the pastor who gave us the barbeque." She began to sing, "I Just Want to Thank You Lord." Tears flowed from my eyes, because I didn't know it was a band I fed. I didn't realize that even the band members get hungry and sometimes have need for shelter. Now every year that same band comes to play for The House of Love Ministries, and they ask nothing in return for their gift. They are also honorary members of the House of Love Ministries; they call me for prayer when in crisis and before they record albums.

This next story is another mighty move by God. I was outside working at the concession stand next to the church when a man walked up and asked if he could speak to me. I invited him into the church, where I always keep the music soft and ready for prayer or confessions. This man began to cry as he talked to me, saying how much we blessed him by the newspaper articles of all the baptisms we were having. We had been placing how many baptisms, along with the names, in the local newspaper. The Holy Spirit told me to do this. If someone gets arrested *his* name is in the paper, so why not publish people's names when they become a new person in Christ? To date we have 170 baptisms.

This man went on to make his confession to me. He said that he was performing with several other bands in Celina, Ohio. After the performance, all the performers were praying together, when one member stood and said God told him to play for The House of Love in Paulding, Ohio. Simultaneously, five other people stood, all from different bands, and said God told them the same thing. They knew that this was an act of God, it was not rehearsed or choreographed, and being obedient to the Holy Spirit, they gathered all their equipment together in a rented truck and were on their way at that moment.

The band arrived that night at about nine. It was after one-thirty in the morning when they got all of their equipment set up. They returned on Sunday at three in the afternoon to be our praise and worship band. We called them "The Band of Love." This band could perform for us one Sunday a month. Because of the member's affiliations with other musicians and family members who were also musicians, one band soon became two. We called them "The Love Band."

Now with the bands in place, and all our prayers being answered by God; there was one small dilemma. We found that there was resistance in giving God praise. The two different bands had two totally different sounds. One sounded like a Christian rock band, and the other had more of a worship sound. The people that were present still lacked the ability to express themselves through praise and worship. I thought perhaps I could lead the praise and worship off with an exciting intro, or by clapping my hands in the air to the beat; anything to get the congregation to follow. Sometimes they would just stare at me while the music was playing and the words of the songs were displayed on the screen. I thought, "Lord, do I have a church of zombies?"

I would hit the pulpit running, all fired up, trying to motivate souls with the Word of God. It was frustrating to me because I would ask the congregation to call the name of

Jesus, and as I looked around the room, very few would actually call out His name. Sometimes I'd even say, "On the count of three, I want everyone to call the name of Jesus" and still some mouths remained closed. I felt like Moses at times; remember when he hit the rock? I didn't want to become angry at God's people because they were not responding the way *I* thought they should. I just didn't understand it. I knew God had touched me in a way that was inexpressible and sometimes unspeakable. All I could do is weep. Other times I could just shout, and at times, I could break and run.

Our membership has since matured to the extent that there are a few more amen's and a few more hand claps. However you just wait until the revival, wait till they feel the Holy Spirit, they'll shout and run and clap and cry, HALLELUIA!!!

Chapter 18

Adding It All Up

MY AWAKENING OCCURRED many years ago when God slayed me in the spirit and I received the baptism of the Holy Spirit. After I was slain in the spirit, God restored all that was lost along the journey. There is a process to receiving blessing from God. Being steadfast is holding onto these blessings with thanksgiving and gratitude. Do not forget or throw them back in God's face. Continuing to make Jesus Christ the center of our lives keeps us walking in the Spirit. Harken to His voice. Building a relationship with Christ assures we are always listening to his voice and to his instructions. Rejoice in the Lord. Be happy the way you are in the Lord. Believe in God and Jesus Christ. Believe you have been called in His Word. Believe in everlasting life. Most of all, believe in Heaven and eternity with Him.

Why God kept using me, I will never know. I kept working for Him. I would find myself speaking to, and loving on every passerby. Sometimes I would get very angry; if I had not spoken to them first, they would have not spoken to me. Anyway, I kept speaking and loving on them. Because of that; I have met and forged some great relationships with the people of Paulding, Ohio. I have also lead many people to Christ.

To my surprise, every one that I met and ministered to was just like me, in need of God's love and mercy. I remember working through the pain and anguish of perceived racism. Sometimes it seemed no matter what I did, it was never good enough. The other churches always had more money, more people and more participation. It always seemed that I was working the hardest. I would get angry because we spent so much money on this ministry, and still we are called fools. Sometimes I would hear the rumors and lies that were spoken regarding me. I even became desperate at times for kudos and accolades. I have often battled with flesh because I wanted acknowledgement for all the work I had done in this community, serving God.

In Spiritual mediation, I had to realize that His Grace was sufficient for me. Jesus Christ went through so much more, to the point of death by crucifixion for you and I. The Holy Spirit gave me comfort through a quote by Mother Teresa, Now Saint Teresa, "People are often unreasonable and self-centered; FORGIVE THEM ANYWAY: If you are kind, people might accuse you of ulterior motives; BE KIND ANYWAY: If you are honest, people may cheat you; BE HONEST ANYWAY: If you find happiness, people may be jealous; BE HAPPY ANYWAY: The good you do today may be forgotten tomorrow; DO GOOD ANYWAY: Give the world the best that you have, and it may never be enough; GIVE YOUR BEST ANYWAY: For you see, in the end, it is between YOU AND GOD; It was never between you and them anyway."

> *For by grace are ye saved through faith; and that not of yourselves: it is the gift of God: Not of works, lest any man should boast.*
> Ephesians 2:8-9 (KJV)

I don't know why God chose me to come to Paulding, Ohio to start this ministry and do his work, but I am so glad He did. Along the way I have met so many beautiful, loving, God fearing people. As much as I would have liked to have been more obedient, more holy, more perfect, more prepared, and more equipped; I was not. Time after time, Christ reminded me that His strength is made perfect in our weakness. I always wanted to be more, but He always wanted me to be less. The first shall be last, and the last shall be first. The most perfect thing that I have seen on this assignment, this journey, is that God's mercy endures forever. God chooses to have mercy on those he chooses to have mercy.

> *Therefore God has mercy on whom he wants to have mercy, and he hardens whom he wants to harden.*
>
> Romans 9:18 (NIV)

In my case, while building the House of Love, He chose mercy.

The End

Special Thanks

To my sisters; Gladys Shannon, Robin Bell, Tracy Richardson, and Aleta or "Letha" Jones; may you rest in peace. You were all the best sisters a brother could have.

To my brother-in-law, William (Wild Bill) Bell; may you rest in peace.

To, Tom and Kim Sinn, Larry and Becky Fishbaugh Jeramiah and Stephanie Leroy, Greg and Beth Griffiths, Al and Cheri Griffith, Dan and Jill Straley, Rick Grear, and so many others who have sown seeds into the House of Love Ministry. Thank You!

Thanks to Allie Brown for putting my thoughts on paper.

To Jane Neice for the first edit.

CPSIA information can be obtained
at www.ICGtesting.com
Printed in the USA
FFOW02n1416301017
41706FF

9 781545 609415